W9-ARB-684

NUMBER TWENTY-SIX:

The Walter Prescott Webb Memorial Lectures

Essays on
The American Civil Rights Movement

[THE WALTER PRESCOTT WEBB MEMORIAL LECTURES]

Essays on The American Civil Rights Movement

BY JOHN DITTMER, GEORGE C. WRIGHT,
AND W. MARVIN DULANEY

Introduction by Clayborne Carson
Edited by W. Marvin Dulaney
and Kathleen Underwood

Published for the University of Texas at Arlington by
Texas A&M University Press : College Station

WINGATE COLLEGE LIBRARY

Copyright © 1993 by the University of Texas at Arlington
Manufactured in the United States of America
All rights reserved
First edition

The paper used in this book meets the minimum requirements
of the American National Standard for Permanence
of Paper for Printed Library Materials, Z39.48–1984.
Binding materials have been chosen for durability.
♾

Library of Congress Cataloging-in-Publication Data

Dittmer, John, 1939–
Essays on the American civil rights movement / by John Dittmer, George C. Wright, and W. Marvin Dulaney ; introduction by Clayborne Carson ; edited by W. Marvin Dulaney and Kathleen Underwood. — 1st ed.
p. cm. — (The Walter Prescott Webb memorial lectures ; no. 26)
ISBN 0-89096-540-4
1. Afro-Americans — Civil rights — Southern States. 2. Civil rights movements — Southern States — History — 20th century. 3. Southern States — Race relations. I. Wright, George C. II. Dulaney, W. Marvin, 1950– . III. Underwood, Kathleen, 1944– . IV. Title. V. Series: Walter Prescott Webb memorial lectures ; 26.
E185.615.D58 1993
323.1'196073075 — dc20 92-45792
CIP

To Edward W. Chester

Contents

Preface

THE CIVIL RIGHTS MOVEMENT is one of the most significant movements in American history. Like a well-acted morality play, the civil rights movement changed American society from one that tolerated racism and the subjugation of African Americans to one that recognized the rights and humanity of all its citizens regardless of color or race. The issues raised by the civil rights movement also stimulated a new era of democracy and freedom in American society. Both the modern women's movement and the antiwar movement of the 1960s were stimulated by the civil rights movement. In fact, some Americans participated in all three of the great movements of the 1960s and even employed the strategies and tactics of mass organizing and civil disobedience so prevalent in the civil rights movement in the latter movements.

Given the importance of the civil rights movement as a major force in shaping modern American society, it was quite appropriate that the 1991 Walter Prescott Webb Memorial Lectures focused on this era in American history. This volume contains the papers presented at the twenty-sixth annual lecture series held at the University of Texas at Arlington. The lectures presented by John Dittmer, George C. Wright, and W. Marvin Dulaney followed a basic theme: how participants in the civil rights movement sought to end racism, racial discrimination, and segregation through mass organizing, direct action, lawsuits, participation in politics, and negotiation. While the locales for the movement may have varied, in their quest for equal rights and social justice, the participants in the civil rights movement used essentially the same strategies and tactics.

The scholars in this volume have made significant contributions to the field of African-American history. In addition, two are nationally recognized scholars for their work on the civil rights movement. Clayborne Carson, who introduces the volume, is professor of history and director/editor of the Martin Luther King, Jr., Paper Project at

Stanford University. He has published *In Struggle: SNCC and the Black Awakening of the 1960s* and *Malcolm X: The FBI File.*

John Dittmer is professor of history and chair of the Department of History at DePauw University in Indiana. He has published *Black Georgia in the Progressive Era* and served as a consultant on the award-winning documentary series on the civil rights movement, "Eyes on the Prize."

George C. Wright is professor of history and vice-provost at the University of Texas, Austin. He has published articles in the *Journal of Negro History, Journal of American History,* and the *Filson Club Quarterly.* He has published two books on African-American history in Kentucky: *Life behind a Veil: Blacks in Louisville, Kentucky, 1865–1930,* and *Racial Violence in Kentucky, 1865–1940: Lynchings, Mob Rule and "Legal Lynchings."*

W. Marvin Dulaney is assistant professor of history at the University of Texas at Arlington and co-editor of this volume. He has published articles on African-American history in Texas in *Legacies* and the *Houston Review.* His first book, *Black Police in America,* is forthcoming.

Kathleen Underwood is co-editor of this volume and associate professor of history at the University of Texas at Arlington. She is a social historian of the American West and has published *Town Building on the Colorado Frontier.* She also co-edited volume twenty-three of the Webb lecture series, *Essays on Sunbelt Cities and Recent Urban America.*

A number of people contributed to the completion of this volume and the success of the Webb lectures series. The series continues to benefit from the support of C. B. Smith, Sr., an Austin businessman and former student of Walter Prescott Webb who generously established the Webb Endowment Fund and made possible the publication of the lectures. Jenkins and Virginia Garrett have also been perennial supporters of the Webb Lectures. Recently, the Webb lecture series has received major support from the Rudolf Hermanns' Endowment for the Liberal Arts. Webb Committee Chair Stephen Maizlish offered considerable assistance in planning and arranging the lectures. Department head Kenneth R. Philp also offered invaluable leadership and guidance. Harry Robinson of the Dallas Museum of African-American Life and Culture graciously provided financial support for the lectures. President Wendell Nedderman also provided both financial support and the hospitality of his home.

We dedicate this volume to our late colleague and friend Edward W. Chester, who died in the fall of 1990. Professor Chester was a prolific writer, an aficionado of music and theater, and a keen baseball fan. His gruff demeanor hid a kind heart, and we miss him.

W. Marvin Dulaney
Kathleen Underwood

Essays on
The American Civil Rights Movement

CLAYBORNE CARSON

Introduction

THE ESSAYS that follow demonstrate the difficulty of defining boundaries for studies of the civil rights movement. Rather than narrowly focusing on the major civil rights leaders and organizations, the most interesting new work has examined the sometimes ambiguous relationship between leadership at the national level and localized social movements. Civil rights reform has increasingly been seen in the context of broader, long-term changes in American racial relations. Without discounting the importance of the civil rights legislation passed during the 1960s, scholars have also begun to acknowledge that the African-American freedom struggle accomplished more than the elimination of racial barriers. The mass militancy that overturned the Jim Crow system brought about a transformation of traditional social relationships and cultural norms. In addition to changes in the legal status of black Americans, the freedom struggle achieved profound changes in racial consciousness.

The impressive amount of new scholarship appearing in this field suggests the enormous range of possibilities for innovative research. Recent studies of the modern era in African-American politics have devoted less attention to national civil rights leaders and organizations and more to transformations of racial consciousness.[1] Even studies of Martin Luther King, Jr., have become increasingly informed by an understanding of his roots in African-American religious traditions and of his occasionally tenuous ties to the grassroots protest movements that tested his leadership.[2] More generally, the best new work has abandoned a narrow focus on legal and political reform and has begun to examine broader social, cultural, and intellectual themes. The civil rights movement is increasingly understood as related to the long-term development of African-American thought and institutions and as an aspect of ongoing changes in American race relations. The outpouring of recent studies ensures that the field will remain one of the most intellectually exciting areas of historical research.

As scholars have broadened their range of inquiry, they have debated about starting and ending points for their studies. Some accounts of the modern African-American struggle have indicated that it began in 1954 with the Supreme Court's *Brown* v. *Board of Education* decision or with Rosa Parks's refusal in December, 1955, to give up her seat on a Montgomery city bus. Or that it ended with the passage of the 1965 Voting Rights Act or with the assassination of Martin Luther King, Jr. A listing of titles of historical narratives in the field reveals still other chronological boundaries: Robert H. Brisbane, *The Black Vanguard: Origins of the Negro Social Revolution, 1900–1960* (1970); Thomas R. Brooks, *Walls Come Tumbling Down: A History of the Civil Rights Movement, 1940–1970* (1974); Juan Williams, *Eyes on the Prize: American Civil Rights Years, 1954–1965* (1987); Harvard Sitkoff, *The Struggle for Black Equality, 1954–1980* (1981).

The tendency to categorize events according to a chronology of nationally significant events is understandable but nonetheless misleading when applied to an era of locally based struggles. As contemporary scholars shift their focus from the handful of civil rights events that received national press coverage to analyses of movements in particular communities, they have employed a variety of appropriate chronological frameworks. William Chafe, *Civilities and Civil Rights: Greensboro, North Carolina, and the Black Struggle for Freedom* (1980); David R. Colburn, *Racial Change and Community Crisis: St. Augustine, Florida, 1877–1980* (1985); and Robert J. Norrell, *Reaping the Whirlwind: The Civil Rights Movement in Tuskegee* (1985), each demonstrated continuities linking the pre-*Brown* era with the years after King's assassination.

Studies that examine the civil rights movement in particular localities reveal that each movement has a distinctive history. The narratives by Chafe, Colburn, and Norrell are shaped by local rather than national events and reflect the idiosyncratic characteristics of local rather than national leaders and groups. In the three communities investigated by these scholars, King and other nationally known civil rights leaders played only minor roles in the sustained movements that occurred. The daily lives of residents of these communities were affected as much by concessions gained from local white officials and from the development of local movement institutions as by passage of the 1964 Civil Rights Act and the 1965 Voting Rights Act. Rather than assuming that localized mass movements sought to fall in line with a national agenda of civil rights legislation, community studies raise questions about the complex interactions between local and national concerns. They remind us that the most important changes in race relations during the period after World War II have been those which affected the everyday lives of African Americans and altered or transformed their world views.

The states and communities discussed in this collection of essays became the settings for unique movements that reflected geographically specific patterns of race relations. For example, in the first essay John Dittmer examines the Mississippi Freedom Democratic party (MFDP), one of the most important and distinctive institutional manifestations of the African-American struggle in the deep South. As Dittmer points out, the MFDP's movement origins infused it with radical ideas that extended beyond the ideological boundaries of conventional liberalism. Seeking to assess the impact of grass-roots activism on the Mississippi political structure, he describes the unsuccessful effort of activists affiliated with the Student Nonviolent Coordinating Committee and the Congress of Racial Equality to take control of Mississippi's Democratic party. Dittmer demonstrates how "moderate" black and white leaders were able to prevail over radicals as militancy gave way to the accommodation of the late 1960s.

George C. Wright's study notes that in Kentucky, as elsewhere in the South, the Jim Crow system had become institutionalized by the early years of the twentieth century, but some aspects of Kentucky's segregationist system and the black struggle to change that system were distinctive. As in other border states, Kentucky's colleges and universities were desegregated even before the *Brown* decision, and public school integration began in the late 1950s when massive resistance was being practiced elsewhere in the South. Although Wright does not explicitly contrast Kentucky's pattern of race relations with that of other states, his study provides a basis for such comparisons. Comparative studies of the desegregation process are needed in order to determine the extent to which variables such as obstinacy of white officials and the militancy of black activists determined the pace of racial reform.

W. Marvin Dulaney's account of the civil rights movement in

Dallas echoes Dittmer's observations regarding the positive long-term consequences of mass activism. Dulaney demonstrates that "a general pattern of apartheid" existed in Dallas, despite its location in a state that is often considered outside the South. Tracing African-American advancement movements from the 1930s through the 1970s, he notes the continuing tension between black advocates of militancy and confrontation and those who relied on conciliation and negotiation. His discussion of the process of desegregation in Dallas during the 1960s indicates that the less assertive tactics were not as effective in achieving change as the more aggressive tactics would have been. As a result of the decision of black leaders to abjure mass protest activities, he concludes, "a legacy of apathy exists among the city's African-American population and it has forestalled mobilizing them even for causes and issues which directly affect them."

Taken together, the essays in this volume point out that different concepts of chronological boundaries in civil rights studies closely relate to alternative conceptions of the nature of the field itself. The most significant recent works on the civil rights movement have demonstrated that a full understanding of modern African-American political life requires an interdisciplinary perspective and a broad notion of the relevant factors to be explained. Sociologist Aldon D. Morris's *The Origins of the Civil Rights Movement: Black Communities Organizing for Change* (1984), for example, has clarified the role of preexisting institutions in preparing the way for the mass protests of the 1960s. Although he focuses on Martin Luther King, Jr., Taylor Branch in his Pulitzer prize–winning *Parting the Waters* similarly deepens our understanding of the social roots and diverse leadership of the modern African-American freedom struggle.

Narrowly understood, the civil rights movement was an effort to achieve national civil rights reform, but it involved much more than that. Like any social movement, it generated emergent norms and values. Civil rights reforms removed barriers to the freedom of African Americans, but the transformation of racial consciousness symbolized by the Black Power slogan affected many blacks as much as did changes in legal rights. Participants were transformed in profound ways through their experiences in a sustained social struggle. They assumed new roles and aspirations as they lived within movement communities. Small-scale protests to end segregation in public facilities and to achieve new civil rights legislation became a mass movement to alter all aspects of black-white relations. Discontent with the status quo in race relations fostered intellectual ferment within black communities and ultimately brought about a profound transformation in African-American political and cultural consciousness. The modern civil rights movement, which struggled to break down racial barriers, evolved into an African-American freedom struggle seeking to raise fundamental questions about race and destiny.

By transforming the consciousness of black participants, African-American struggles marked a major historical turning point. Perhaps the most important area of future research, therefore, is the relationship between modern African-American movements and the varied movements that continue to transform the world during an era in which class-conscious movements have had a declining significance. Important recent studies have linked the black movement to the emergence of a modern women's liberation movement and to other identity-based movements.[3] Such studies remind us of the fact that African-American movements have always been a stimulus for broadly based movements to expand conceptions of freedom and democracy beyond the restricted ideological boundaries that would have prevailed otherwise.

NOTES

1. Cf. Clayborne Carson, *In Struggle: SNCC and the Black Awakening of the 1960s* (Cambridge: Harvard University Press, 1981); Aldon D. Morris, *The Origins of the Civil Rights Movement: Black Communities Organizing for Change* (New York: Free Press, 1984); George Lipsitz, *A Life in the Struggle: Ivory Perry and the Culture of Opposition* (Philadelphia: Temple University Press, 1988); James H. Cone, *Martin & Malcolm & America: A Dream or a Nightmare* (Maryknoll, N.Y.: Orbis Books, 1991). For a survey of this literature, see Martin Luther King, Jr., Papers Project, *A Guide to Research on Martin Luther King, Jr., and the Modern Black Freedom Struggle* (Stanford: Stanford University Libraries, 1989).

2. Cf. David L. Lewis, *King: A Critical Biography* (New York: Praeger, 1970); Stephen B. Oates, *Let the Trumpet Sound: The Life of Martin Luther King, Jr.* (New York: Harper & Row, 1982); David J. Garrow, *Bearing the Cross: Martin Luther King and the Southern Christian Leadership Conference* (New York: William Morrow & Co., 1986); Taylor Branch, *Parting the Waters: America in the King Years, 1954–63* (New York: Simon & Schuster, 1988); Lewis V. Baldwin, *There Is a Balm in Gilead: The Cultural Roots of Martin Luther King, Jr.* (Minneapolis: Fortress Press, 1991).

3. See, for example, Sara Evans, *Personal Politics: The Roots of Women's Libera-*

tion in the Civil Rights Movement and the New Left (New York: Vintage Books, 1979); Mary King, *Freedom Song: A Personal Story of the 1960s Civil Rights Movement* (New York: William Morrow & Co., 1986); and Michael Omi and Howard Winant, *Racial Formation in the United States: From the 1960s to the 1980s* (New York: Routledge & Kegan Paul, 1986).

JOHN DITTMER

The Transformation of the Mississippi Movement, 1964–68: The Rise and Fall of the Freedom Democratic Party

THANKS to the excellent documentary series "Eyes on the Prize" and a misguided movie called *Mississippi Burning*, the civil rights movement in Mississippi has, over the past several years, once again become a subject of interest and study. For most Americans, Mississippi in the 1960s evokes dramatic scenes of courage and confrontation: James Meredith facing down the Oxford mob to enroll at Ole Miss; the haunting posters of James Chaney, Michael Schwerner, and Andrew Goodman, lynched by the Ku Klux Klan in Neshoba County; the eloquent voice of Fannie Lou Hamer, testifying at the Democratic National Convention in Atlantic City. Yet, with the exception of the Meredith March of 1966, during which Stokely Carmichael and Willie Ricks shocked the nation with their call for Black Power, students of history have paid scant attention to the black struggle for freedom in the Magnolia State in the years following the 1964 Summer Project. For in the mid- and late-1960s a series of tumultuous events crowded Mississippi off center stage: urban insurrections in northern ghettoes; the assassinations of Malcolm X, Martin Luther King, Jr., and Robert Kennedy; and above all, America's deepening involvement in Vietnam. But the movement did not die out in Mississippi. African Americans there continued to press their demands for desegregation of public facilities, including schools; equal employment opportunity; and an end to the police and Klan violence that had been the hallmark of the closed society. Above all, the movement sought political power for black Mississippians through a new organization, the Mississippi Freedom Democratic party.

Since the formation of the first National Association for the Advancement of Colored People (NAACP) branch in 1918 in Vicksburg, obtaining the vote had been the primary goal of black activists in Mississippi. The state constitution of 1890 had effectively disfranchised Mississippi blacks, then over half the population, through the poll tax and a series of amendments requiring that applicants demonstrate an "understanding" of the state constitution. Local registrars routinely failed black applicants while registering all whites. As a result, few blacks even attempted to register until World War II. Then, in 1944, The United States Supreme Court, in the *Smith* v. *Allwright* decision, outlawed the Democrats' white primary, the only election of importance in the South. Believing that the federal government was now on their side, blacks across the South mounted voter registration drives. In Mississippi, returning World War II veterans led the campaign, which was met with white hostility and violence.[1]

By 1954 only twenty-two thousand blacks were registered to vote, 4 percent of those eligible. That same year *Brown* v. *Board of Education* declared segregated public schools unconstitutional, and black Mississippians, again emboldened by a Supreme Court action, filed school desegregation petitions and organized groups of people to take the registration test. The leader of this movement was the NAACP's first state field secretary in Mississippi, Medgar Evers. A World War II veteran, Evers crisscrossed the state to organize NAACP chapters, line up local people to file school desegregation petitions, and persuade eligible blacks to try to register to vote. White Mississippi responded as it had in the past. The newly formed Citizens' Council, a group of leading businessmen, employed economic coercion to persuade blacks to remove their names from the school petitions and also threatened citizens attempting to register. If these measures failed, whites resorted to violence to preserve their supremacy. In Belzoni, NAACP branch president Rev. George W. Lee was gunned down by a carload of whites. His friend and fellow activist, Gus Courts, survived an assassination attempt but had to flee the state. And in Brookhaven a sixty-year-old farmer named Lamar Smith, a leader of the registration campaign, was shot and killed on the courthouse lawn in broad daylight. There were no convictions in any of these cases.[2]

These politically inspired crimes, along with the lynching of young Emmett Till for allegedly whistling at a white woman, led one white Mississippian to conclude that "There's open season on Negroes now.

. . . Any peckerwood who wants can go shoot himself one, and we'll free him. Our situation will get worse and worse." The combination of economic intimidation and physical violence had dealt a severe blow to movement efforts in Mississippi. Local NAACP branches reported membership losses, and fear of white reprisal forced a number of key activists to move away from the state. The Eisenhower administration did little or nothing to enforce the U.S. Constitution in Mississippi. Medgar Evers worked feverishly to keep the movement alive, giving pep talks and attempting to allay fears through his own example. But the results were not heartening. By the end of the decade the movement was at a standstill: there were even fewer blacks registered to vote than there had been in 1954.[3]

The second wave of the Mississippi movement began with the Freedom Rides in 1961 and ended at the Democratic National Convention in Atlantic City in the summer of 1964. In many ways this new burst of activism was consistent with the initial stirrings of the 1950s. Older, middle-class leaders supplied the base for movement activities in their communities, feeding and housing civil rights workers and offering them a degree of protection. The basic thrust of the movement remained, as it had been for nearly a century, that of voter registration. Still, the contrasts between the two decades are striking. The movement of the 1950s had been based in the cities, dominated by the NAACP, and centered around the small black middle class. (Few black sharecroppers signed school petitions or were encouraged to register and vote.)

Organizers in the 1960s, on the other hand, saw the rural poor as their natural constituency. Young activists abandoned coats and ties for denim overalls in a symbolic effort to identify with the majority of the state's black citizens. And where in the 1950s black men had dominated local leadership, now women were entering the movement in larger numbers. They became the backbone of the struggle, forming a majority at most mass meetings and participating in all phases of activity, from running for Congress to serving time in prison. While the new movement did not succeed in eliminating all distinctions of class and gender, it came closer to the ideal of the egalitarian community than has any major American social movement, before or since.[4]

The most visible change in the 1960s was the influx of newcomers. The southern sit-ins in 1960 inspired black men and women in their teens and twenties to commit themselves to work full time in Mississippi. A number of these activists were affiliated with the Congress of Racial Equality (CORE), but most were organizers with the Student Nonviolent Coordinating Committee (SNCC), which began its Mississippi operations in McComb in the summer of 1961. The Southern Christian Leadership Conference (SCLC) made no major commitment but did establish leadership schools to assist in the registration effort. The NAACP, with Medgar Evers as field secretary and Aaron Henry, a Clarksdale druggist, as state president, remained active in several communities. The presence of these different protest groups would eventually create interorganizational problems, but until Atlantic City, tensions were kept under control, in part because of the establishment in early 1962 of the Conference of Federated Organizations. COFO represented an honest, and for the most part successful, effort to unify all national, state, and local movement organizations operating in Mississippi. SNCC's Bob Moses was named director of COFO's voter registration work, with CORE's Dave Dennis as assistant director. Aaron Henry of the NAACP was COFO president, but from the outset SNCC supplied most of COFO's organizers and financial support and quickly emerged as the dominant partner in the coalition.[5]

During the first eighteen months of its existence, COFO organized in black communities across the northern half of the state. SNCC concentrated its voter registration drive in the Delta city of Greenwood, attracting national attention as police brutally repressed local people attempting to gain the franchise. CORE's activities centered in Madison County, located just north of the capital city of Jackson, and in Meridian, on the Alabama border. Operating out of his home base in Clarksdale, Aaron Henry combined voter registration with a boycott of that city's white businesses, which refused to desegregate their facilities or employ blacks in other than menial positions. And in Jackson, a similar NAACP campaign ended tragically with the assassination of Medgar Evers, shot from ambush as he arrived home after addressing a mass meeting.

Despite the dedication of movement activists and the courage of thousands of black Mississippians, by the end of the summer of 1963 the movement was stalled on every front. Whites simply refused to register black applicants or negotiate movement demands and kept their jails full of "troublemakers." The Kennedy administration, while identifying with the goals of the activists, had offered little more than token support. Some twenty lawsuits involving discrimination against black voter registrants, which had been filed by the Justice Department, had gotten bogged down in the courts. FBI agents, often at the scene when blacks were beaten and arrested while peacefully picketing, made no arrests, claiming they lacked jurisdiction. The Kennedy policy here was "Federalism," with its basic premise that "the responsibility for the preservation of law and order . . . is the responsibility of local authorities." Only when a situation deteriorated to the point where local officials could not (or would not) control it — as when James Meredith enrolled at the University of Mississippi — would the federal government respond with outside force.[6] Thus after three years of organizing, civil rights workers in Mississippi had made few tangible gains, and most whites felt they could crush the movement without fear of federal intervention. If black activists were to find a way to organize their communities, they had to change tactics.

That new strategy took shape in the summer of 1963 with a COFO decision to hold a statewide mock election and culminated in the challenge of the Mississippi Freedom Democratic party at the Democratic National Convention in August of 1964. The "freedom vote's" purposes were twofold: to demonstrate that, given an opportunity, large numbers of blacks would participate in the political process and to attract national attention to the brutal repression that accompanied efforts by blacks to gain their rights. COFO nominated NAACP state president Aaron Henry for governor and Edwin King, white chaplain at Tougaloo College, for lieutenant governor. The freedom vote was a success. More than eighty thousand blacks (and a handful of whites) cast ballots for the Henry-King ticket, despite widespread harassment.

The national media, however, took little interest in the campaign, and the pattern of repression in Mississippi continued into 1964. By then, COFO had made plans for a summer project that brought hundreds of northern volunteers, most of whom were white college students, into the state to work on voter registration, in community centers, and in the new freedom schools established to provide black children with basic skills and an understanding of African-American history. The volunteers also assisted in the organization of the Freedom Democratic party (FDP), which would send a delegation to the national convention to challenge the seating of the all-white segregationist regular delegation.[7]

When the Mississippi Freedom Democratic Party held its state convention in Jackson on August 6, nearly twenty-five hundred people packed into the Masonic Temple. Several northern state delegations had pledged to support the FDP challenge, and Washington attorney Joseph Rauh, who had strong connections to the Democratic party's liberal wing, had signed on as legal counsel to guide FDP through the bureaucratic maze of convention regulations. Rauh explained the process to the delegates assembled in Jackson: FDP would first take its case to the credentials committee, arguing that blacks had been excluded from the regular party and that FDP was the only party in the state loyal to the national ticket. Should the committee refuse to seat FDP, then all it would take to bring the issue to the convention floor—where the issue could be raised before a national television audience—would be for 11 members of the 108-person credentials committee and eight state delegations to support the FDP position. Should the issue be decided by the convention as a whole, Rauh assured his Jackson audience, the chances for success would be excellent.[8]

The major task at the Jackson meeting was to elect delegates to the national convention. Earlier in the day Ella Baker, a veteran movement warrior and SNCC advisor, had warned her audience, "We must be careful lest we elect to represent us people who, for the first time, feel their sense of importance and will represent themselves before they represent you."[9] Baker was aware that during the past month traditional NAACP leaders had decided that although they had not been active in organizing the FDP or in planning the challenge, now that it was a reality they should occupy a prominent place in the delegation. These men (the establishment leadership was male) had been active in earlier registration campaigns, but their approach to social change was gradualist, and they had been guarded in their dealings with the young activists in SNCC and CORE. Yet now that the train had arrived and was getting ready to pull out, these established leaders scrambled to get on board. FDP organizers worked behind the scenes to keep as many of them as possible standing at the station.

Bob Moses later recalled that he and other COFO activists wanted to get "as radical a delegation as you could, people who would stand up when they got to Atlantic City." Thus at the FDP convention in

Jackson—where the majority of the sixty-eight-person delegation was to be selected—organizers took steps to make sure the Atlantic City contingent represented the black majority, the rural poor. To do so, it was necessary to engage in old-style politics, with COFO staff members distributing a slate of delegates to be elected at large. The balloting divided roughly along rural and urban lines, with representatives from the countryside uniting to elect their people and to defeat "big city" businessmen and professionals. Middle-class leaders were by no means excluded from the delegation—they would make their presence felt at Atlantic City during the debate. But the FDP delegation as a whole was militant and included such grassroots activists as E. W. Steptoe, Winson Hudson, Hazel Palmer, and Fannie Lou Hamer—local people with little formal education or social status, but who spoke from experience in the name of the dispossessed.[10]

Held during the last week of August, the Democratic National Convention was to be a coronation of sorts for Pres. Lyndon B. Johnson. No other names were to be placed in nomination; there would be no major platform fights. A week before the convention the only item of suspense was Johnson's choice for a running mate. But the sixty-four blacks and four whites who comprised the Mississippi Freedom Democratic party delegation upset the president's plans for an orchestrated convention.

The FDP delegates arrived in Atlantic City by bus the day before the all-important hearing with the credentials committee. Housed in the small, run-down Gem Hotel, about a mile from the convention hall, These Mississippians stood in sharp contrast to the well-heeled rank-and-file party faithful. Sharecroppers and small landowners, maids and mechanics, schoolteachers and middle-class business owners, the Freedom Party delegation accurately reflected the socioeconomic composition of the state's black population. SNCC worker Mary King recalls that the delegates were at first "dazzled and bewildered by the scene, and by the media attention they immediately attracted." But they quickly got down to business, fanning out over the convention grounds, buttonholing delegates, bringing them the word on life in Mississippi and the righteousness of the challenge.

Although the FDP delegates were objects of interest and curiosity at a convention that promised to be dull, few political observers had taken their challenge seriously. A week earlier, Mississippi governor

Paul Johnson had told the press that the president had assured him that the Freedom Democrats would not be seated. Now that the Republicans had nominated Sen. Barry Goldwater, the Arizona senator who had voted against the 1964 Civil Rights Bill, Lyndon Johnson was confident of his base among black voters but feared a white blacklash in the South if the FDP gained recognition. More immediately, Johnson was concerned that southern delegations might walk out of the convention if FDP were seated.[11]

Whatever chances FDP had, depended on the credentials committee hearings. Here both FDP and the regulars would present their cases before a jury of 108 Democrats. Since this committee was dominated by the president's supporters, no one expected it to act favorably on the challenge. But the FDP strategy remained the same as outlined earlier by attorney Joe Rauh: if 10 percent of the committee — 11 members — filed a minority report supporting FDP, that report would come to the convention floor. And if eight states then requested a roll call, every delegation would have to go on record, avoiding the voice-vote rubber stamp that convention chairs so often used to decide unpopular issues. Going into the credentials committee meeting, Rauh was confident that he had his "eleven and eight" with room to spare.

When committee chair David Lawrence gaveled the meeting to order, network cameras were there to cover the proceedings live. White Mississippians defended their delegation's loyalty, pointing to the support Mississippi had given the party's presidential nominees in the past. And they denied that blacks had difficulty voting in the Magnolia State. The challengers argued that FDP should be seated because blacks had been shut out of the Mississippi Democratic party. The Freedom party had observed all party regulations in selecting its delegation and had pledged loyalty to the national ticket, while the regulars, who made no secret of their affinity for Barry Goldwater, would not. But legal arguments counted for little at this hearing, which reached its high point with the dramatic, emotional testimony of the former sharecropper from Ruleville, Fannie Lou Hamer.[12]

The several million Americans who watched the proceedings live on television had known little if anything about Mrs. Hamer, but as she graphically described her life, her eviction from the plantation when she registered to vote, and, most dramatically, her beating in the Winona jail after returning from a voter education workshop in

South Carolina, it immediately became apparent that hers was an authentic voice, describing simply but powerfully the reality of life in the closed society. This was high drama, and it did not go unnoticed in the White House. In the middle of Mrs. Hamer's testimony, President Johnson hurriedly called a press conference, and the networks dutifully cut away before she had completed her remarks. Realizing they had been manipulated, and sensing the importance of the story, the networks played back her testimony that night, where a prime time audience heard her emotional conclusion: "If the Freedom Party is not seated now I question America. Is this America, the land of the free and the home of the brave, where we have to sleep with our telephones off the hook because our lives are threatened daily, because we want to live as decent human beings in America?" Immediately after Mrs. Hamer's testimony, telegrams of support began flooding the convention. FDP had won the first round.[13]

In his memoirs Lyndon Johnson makes no mention of the Mississippi challenge, remembering Atlantic City as a "place of surging crowds and thundering cheers." In fact, the president was not only well aware of the FDP's effort to unseat the Mississippi regulars, he was obsessed by it. Throughout the summer Johnson and his aides had been quietly lobbying important northern governors to oppose the challenge, and such efforts intensified on the convention floor. The person given the responsibility for managing this delicate operation was Sen. Hubert Humphrey of Minnesota. In many ways Humphrey was the ideal choice. A liberal with an impressive civil rights record, Humphrey had close ties with Democrats (such as Joe Rauh) who were supporting FDP. Humphrey had good reason to do the president's bidding, for he was the front-runner for the vice-presidential nomination. Word quickly passed that the president would choose Humphrey as his running mate—providing that the senator kept FDP in line. Joe Rauh began feeling the pressure, both from Humphrey and from Walter Reuther, head of the United Auto Workers, for whom Rauh was legal counsel. The president's operatives on the floor began contacting members of the credentials committee, promising political rewards—or punishment—depending upon how they voted on Mississippi. In addition to his standard arm-twisting approach, Lyndon Johnson turned to J. Edgar Hoover for help.[14]

The White House campaign of surveillance and espionage was a

Watergate that worked. In 1976, in the aftermath of the Nixon scandals, the Senate Select Committee to Study Governmental Operations, the Church Committee, summarized the Atlantic City operation with devastating clarity:

> Approximately 30 Special Agents, headed by Assistant Director Cartha ["Deke"] DeLoach, 'were able to keep the White House fully apprised of all major developments during the Convention's course' by means of 'information coverage, by use of various confidential techniques, by infiltration of key groups through use of undercover agents, and through utilization of agents using appropriate cover as reporters'. Among these "confidential techniques" were: a wiretap on the hotel room occupied by Dr. Martin Luther King, Jr., and microphone surveillance of a storefront serving as headquarters for the Student Nonviolent Coordinating Committee and another civil rights organization [CORE].[15]

FBI intelligence gathered at the convention proved valuable. Agents posing as NBC correspondents (the network cooperated) gained off-the-record information through interviews. The wiretaps provided important data on FDP strategy throughout the convention, and FBI agents operated an informant who attended all FDP meetings and caucuses. Correspondence in the Johnson Library reveals a constant stream of memoranda to the president's desk during convention week. DeLoach passed on the FDP reports to Johnson's aides on the floor, Walter Jenkins and Bill Moyers (whose FBI code name for the week was "Bishop"), and they in turn phoned it in to Lee White at the White House, or to Johnson directly.[16]

The veteran SNCC and CORE activists at the convention were fully aware that the White House was working against them, but not even they suspected that to thwart the Freedom Democrats' challenge the president would resort to tactics normally reserved for spies and gangsters. Instead, they went about the business of lining up support for the challenge, while the FDP delegation debated whether to agree to a compromise on the question of seating. It found acceptable a proposal put forward by Rep. Edith Green of Oregon, a credentials committee member. Under the Green initiative, the convention would seat all members of both Mississippi delegations who would pledge loyalty to the party and the presidential ticket, dividing seats proportionally according to the number who signed the oath. FDP leaders knew that since no more than a handful of the regular delegates would do so, the Green plan would in effect exclude the regulars while seating the challengers. For this reason the proposal was unacceptable to Lyndon Johnson.[17]

The growing support for the Freedom Democrats in Atlantic City compelled the Johnson forces to come up with a compromise of their own. Working through the credentials committee subcommittee, chaired by Minnesota attorney general Walter Mondale, a Humphrey protégé, the White House put forth a three-part proposal. First, FDP representatives Aaron Henry and Ed King would be seated as at-large delegates, with the rest of the delegation "welcomed as honored guests of this convention." Second, only those members of the Mississippi regulars who signed a loyalty oath agreeing to support the party's nominees in November would be seated. Finally, the national Democratic party pledged to eliminate racial discrimination in state delegations in all future conventions.[18] Hubert Humphrey called a meeting with Aaron Henry, Ed King, Bob Moses, Rev. Martin Luther King, Jr., and other activists in an attempt to sell the compromise to them. Moses did not favor the proposal, but he, Henry, and Ed King all said that the FDP delegation would have to decide the question. At that point one of Senator Humphrey's aides burst in to say that there was important news on television. Everyone rushed into the next room to hear a bulletin stating that the credentials committee had just approved the two-seat compromise and that this was a great victory for the civil rights forces. A furious Bob Moses, believing he had been sandbagged, shouted at Humphrey "You tricked us!" and stormed past him, slamming the door on the next vice-president of the United States.[19]

The combination of political pressure from the White House and the compromise itself had all but dissolved FDP's support on the credentials committee. There would be no minority report brought to the convention floor, no roll call vote. The Freedom Democrats' response would now have no bearing on the final outcome. But because the Mississippians had become such a potent symbol, administration officials pushed hard to win their agreement, bringing in such civil rights luminaries as Bayard Rustin and Martin Luther King to persuade FDP to accept the compromise. (King did not employ his considerable oratorical skills to sway the delegation but did say that Humphrey "promised me there would be a new day in Mississippi if you accept this proposal.") An initial FDP response was to stage a sit-in on the convention floor, temporarily occupying the seats of the Mississippi delegation, now all but empty since only four of the regulars agreed to the loyalty oath.[20]

When the Freedom Democrats met for the last time to discuss their position on the compromise, the delegation divided essentially along socioeconomic lines. Bob Moses recalled that the delegates favoring the compromise were largely oriented toward the NAACP, the "more established people from the large cities." Fannie Lou Hamer described this group more graphically: "Everybody that would compromise in five minutes was the people with a real good education. . . . Them folks will sell you—they will sell your mama, their mama, anybody else for a dollar." These were traditional Democrats, who believed that FDP had made its point and now must follow the dictates of their party. Opponents pointed out that the compromise recognized the legitimacy of the racist white delegation; that if King and Henry took the seats, they would be registered as at-large delegates and would not represent Mississippi; and that the Johnson forces did not have the right to decide who the FDP delegates would be. The promise that things would be different in 1968 seemed empty since only a handful of blacks could vote in Mississippi. Aside from these particulars, the grass-roots contingent was furious that the compromise proposal had been sprung on them after the fact and that the people whom they had trusted appeared to have sold them out. In the end it was again Fannie Lou Hamer who stated the case most directly: "I got up and I soon said what I had to say and I sat down. I said, we didn't come all the way up here to compromise for no more than we'd gotten here. . . . We didn't come all this way for no two seats." After hours of discussion and debate, the FDP delegation rejected the Atlantic City compromise.[21]

"For many people," observed SNCC's Joyce Ladner, "Atlantic City was the end of innocence." Bob Moses believed that "Atlantic City was a watershed in the movement, because up until then the idea had been that you were working more or less within the Democratic Party. We were working with them on voting, other things like that. With Atlantic City, a lot of movement people became disillusioned. . . . You turned around and your support was puddle-deep." SNCC's Cleveland Sellers expressed that disillusionment: "Never again were we lulled into believing that our task was exposing injustices so that the 'good' people of America could eliminate them. We left Atlantic City with the knowledge that the movement had turned into something else. After Atlantic City, our struggle was not for civil rights, but for liberation."[22]

For most black Mississippians in the fall of 1964, "liberation" meant working within the system to gain political power. In a decision that surprised many outsiders, early in September members of the executive committee of the FDP voted to endorse and campaign for the Johnson-Humphrey ticket. They argued that "support for Johnson will help in the fight against the Regular Democratic Party," believing "despite Atlantic City, in the ultimate ability of the Democratic Party to meet the challenge of the FDP and eliminate racism from its ranks." This move did not sit well with a number of SNCC and CORE workers. For them the lesson of Atlantic City was that the Democrats could not be trusted; blacks must organize independently of the national party. Yet these staff members were reluctant to impose their will on the new party and its indigenous leadership, for "letting the people decide" was the cornerstone of movement philosophy. Moreover, support for Lyndon Johnson's reelection was but part of a larger freedom vote campaign that featured black candidates running for Congress. FDP's goal, then, was to demonstrate support for the national party while at the same time developing increased political consciousness among black Mississippians.[23]

Spearheading this effort was FDP chair Lawrence Guyot. For the next four years Guyot was the driving force behind the Freedom party. A strong, forceful person whose vocabulary matched his imposing physical stature, Guyot developed a loyal following and bitter enemies within the movement. His credentials were impressive. The Tougaloo College graduate had been in the early contingent of SNCC activists who moved into Greenwood. In 1963 he had been brutally beaten by Winona police, and the following year he had worked closely with local people in organizing black Hattiesburg. A person of unsurpassed physical courage, Guyot was also headstrong and combative, traits that served him better confronting sheriffs than dealing with the subtleties of movement politics.[24]

The 1964 Freedom Vote campaign was a disappointment for FDP and symptomatic of a general malaise that had settled over the Mississippi movement. Approximately sixty thousand blacks cast ballots, down by more than 25 percent from the 1963 vote. White harassment was part of the problem, but the major difficulties were internal. Lawrence Guyot later looked back on this period as one of missed opportunities: "That was a crucial time. We had jolted the country. The state of Mississippi was on the defensive." Instead of maintaining the pressure, the campaign resulted in "utter chaos. . . . For three months there was nothing but anger, frustration. . . . The organizers—between 200 and 300 of them—were completely disillusioned. . . . They would have been better absent than in Mississippi."[25] While Guyot may have overstated the problem, there is no doubt that the summer project and Atlantic City had taken their toll. Many movement veterans were suffering from what psychiatrist Robert Coles (who had worked in the state during the summer) identified as battle fatigue: "In many ways these young civil rights workers are in a war and exposed to the stresses of warfare." Among the symptoms were fear, anxiety, and depression, and those affected might be expected to "take to heavy drinking or become silent, sulky, uncooperative." Coles concluded that "in such cases the non-violent movement itself may be attacked instead of the segregated society formerly felt to be the enemy."[26]

Throughout the fall and winter of 1964 exhausted SNCC and CORE organizers had to contend with declining morale within their projects, problems exacerbated by the more than one hundred white volunteers who had decided to remain in Mississippi after the end of the summer project. These young men and women were full of enthusiasm and ideas and often confident to the point of arrogance. In such an atmosphere black-white tensions, which had flared during the summer, now exploded. Volunteers who had submitted to organizational discipline during the summer now demanded to be treated as equals and often chafed at what they perceived to be authoritarian conduct by black project directors. In Canton, a white volunteer denounced project director George Raymond: "You're a dictator, a little Caesar; you're everything in the movement I'm against. I'm in the movement to get out guys like you!" (Raymond was a man whose courage and dedication were unsurpassed in the movement. Frustrated by the efforts of the newcomers to set policy, he had suggested that they all take a leave of absence and go home to raise money.)[27] Throughout the state debates over tactics, strategy, involvement of local people, and the chain of command all came down to a matter of "black and white."

The pressures began to take their toll. SNCC and CORE workers who had been in Mississippi for nearly three years now began to move away, some to finish college, others to pursue political activity in other states. Still others, victims of battle fatigue, simply dropped out. COFO leaders Bob Moses and Dave Dennis, the key people in the Mississippi civil rights coalition, drifted in and out of the state, and took little part in the day-to-day operations of the central office. In early 1965 both left the state for good. Without leadership or agreement on a program and beset by black-white tensions, COFO went into decline. The young Mississippi Freedom Democratic party stepped in to fill the vacuum, as it pushed ahead with plans to challenge the legitimacy of the state's congressional delegation.[28]

On December 4, 1964, attorneys for the FDP filed a notice of contest, asserting that the five white Mississippi congressmen should not be seated because blacks had been "systematically and deliberately excluded from the electoral process. . . ." The brief also maintained that Victoria Gray, Annie Devine, and Fannie Lou Hamer, three FDP congressional candidates who had run in the freedom vote election after being denied a place on the official ballot, were entitled to the congressional seats in their respective districts. For the next ten months most FDP resources were directed toward the challenge. Activists organized support groups throughout the country, winning endorsement from SNCC, CORE, and SCLC, among other civil rights organizations. On January 4, 1965, the opening day of Congress, more than 600 black Mississippians came to Washington to lobby for their cause and heard Rep. William Fitts Ryan of New York object to the administration of the oath of office to the Mississippi whites. After a debate, the House seated the Mississippians. But 149 members of Congress voted with the FDP, and the resolution seating the congressmen also stated that FDP could present its case "under the laws governing contested elections."[29]

There followed a complicated, drawn-out parliamentary procedure, which saw more than 150 attorneys coming to Mississippi to take depositions in the case, finally presented to the House in September. The results were the same: the white Mississippians kept their seats. But the Freedom Democratic party had focused national attention on the problems facing blacks attempting to register and vote. Along with the more publicized SCLC campaign in Selma, the congressional challenge assured passage of the 1965 Voting Rights Act. Yet if the challenge revitalized the Mississippi movement by providing it with a new mission and focus, it also revealed the problems that FDP was facing in its determination to steer a course independent of the national Democratic party. As was the case with Atlantic City, the White House vigorously opposed the congressional challenge and took steps to distance itself further from the MFDP.[30] The moderate wing of the civil rights movement was also troubled by what it perceived as the radical direction of the new Mississippi party, as was much of the northern liberal establishment of trade unions, intellectuals, and Democratic office holders. Accustomed to facing the hostility of Mississippi's white segregationists, the Freedom party now found itself under attack from "friends" of the movement.

Liberal support for the congressional challenge was by no means unanimous. The national office of the NAACP agreed that while "it would be a good thing to get rid of the Mississippi Congressmen . . . the NAACP does not endorse the method proposed by the MFDP." Specifically, the NAACP took issue with the provision of the challenge that would seat the three FDP women who ran in the mock election. The Americans for Democratic Action concurred with the NAACP. The symbol and substance of American liberalism, the ADA had on its board such important Atlantic City players as Hubert Humphrey, Walter Reuther, and Joe Rauh. Its position was that "the contention that Mrs. Hamer, Devine, and Gray should be seated in Congress is without legal support and has dangerous implications. They were not elected in any regularly-constituted state election." The ADA, then, would "support the challenge to the Mississippi congressmen *unconnected* with the effort to seat the three ladies. . . ." Concerned that "many of our liberal friends, such as the ADA, are trying to undercut the challenge by saying we don't really have legal grounds . . ." The FDP withdrew its demand that the three women be seated.[31]

But the ADA was still uncomfortable with the Freedom Democrats. After a tour of the South, ADA staff member Curtis Gans recommended that the organization "use whatever influence it has to urge SNCC to abandon the Freedom Democratic orientation of its black belt party as being harmful to the freedom and representation the Negroes seek." At the same time, the ADA should push hard for voting rights legislation, for "quick granting of voting rights will mean quick recruitment by the Democratic Party, which in turn will mean quick scuttling of the Freedom Democratic parties. . . ." In the meantime, Gans advised that the ADA should "assist in a quiet freeze of funds on those projects which have a Freedom Democratic Party orientation." Gans was obviously concerned that the MFDP would not accept national party discipline. He and other cold war liberals were equally uncomfortable with the (untrue) charges that the Mississippi movement had been infiltrated by communists. In a series of widely publicized articles, journalists Rowland Evans and Robert Novak painted the young organizers with a broad red brush: "Whether and to what extent these new activists are Communist infiltrated isn't wholly known. But it's significant that [Bob] Moses was a speaker last week in New York at the annual dinner of the *National Guardian*, a publication widely regarded as the most flamboyant exponent of the Chinese Communist line in this country."[32] This red-baiting was to hurt the MFDP, both with its national constituency and at home, where middle-class blacks associated with the NAACP saw an opportunity to regain the positions of leadership they had lost when SNCC and CORE organizers had first moved onto their turf in 1961.

While the national NAACP office had always distrusted the militants in COFO, local NAACP branches had often welcomed SNCC and CORE organizers into their communities and worked with them under the COFO banner. But in the summer of 1964 the coalition began to unravel. Local NAACP leaders charged that the young activists were undermining the NAACP, renouncing the old guard as Uncle Toms and urging black youths in these communities to identify with the new militancy. Differences in life-style were also a problem. Older blacks were offended at the summer volunteers' informal dress and alarmed by interracial courtships, particularly white women dating black men. By the end of the summer, resentment against the young activists was building in NAACP branches across the state. Tensions reached a peak in Atlantic City, where the vote to reject the compromise divided along class and rural-urban lines. Bob Moses later observed that "the thing that the movement had going for it . . . up until the convention was a unity among the black population about the program and goals. And that was shattered at the convention." The "class thing," Moses concluded, "came to a head at Atlantic City." FDP leader Ed King remembered that "suddenly a real class barrier developed the minute we got back from Atlantic City. The old leadership class refused to work with the Freedom Party," and there developed "a kind of internal feuding within the Negro community from a displaced leadership class to restore itself and take the leadership over from a new class of leaders."[33]

The key defection from the movement coalition was that of Aaron Henry. The Clarksdale druggist and state NAACP president was the most ecumenical of all the veteran leaders, welcoming SNCC and CORE workers into his community, supporting the COFO program. At one point NAACP director of branches Gloster Current had grumbled that COFO had "captured the imagination and most of the time of our state president, who offers little to his own organization except lip service." During the middle of the summer Current had written Charles Evers, who had taken his slain brother's place as state field secretary, that "every effort should be made to encourage Dr. Henry to wean himself away from [COFO]." He concluded ominously, "We shall review our relationship with that organization at the end of the summer."[34] Henry also came under pressure from northern liberals, who persuaded him to favor the two-seat compromise in Atlantic City. (Upset by his delegation's refusal to accept the compromise, Henry left the convention before it had ended.)

Henry had participated in the fall freedom vote, running for senator against John Stennis. But attorney Joe Rauh had convinced him that he "had no right to sit in lieu of Stennis," and Henry had withdrawn from the challenge. Relations between Henry and his COFO comrades grew strained, and early in 1965 with Henry's blessing the state NAACP officially severed its ties with COFO.[35] Now Henry was searching for new allies; he found them among a group of Mississippi whites.

One of the direct consequences of the 1954 *Brown* decision and the subsequent formation of the Citizens' Council was the disappearance of the white moderate. In the late 1950s, those whites opposed to Jim Crow either kept their opinions to themselves or left the state. But by the fall of 1964 the civil rights forces had driven a wedge into the closed society, and voices of moderation again surfaced in the Magnolia State. Sensing that the politics of the future in Mississippi would be interracial, these whites wanted to overthrow the segregationist leadership of the state Democratic party. This is not to say that these men (and a few women) were willing to make common cause with the Freedom Democratic party. They saw FDP as a radical black organization dominated by extremists of the New Left. In their efforts to bring about a new Mississippi, the white moderates kept their distance from the FDP and COFO and courted instead disenchanted black moderates like Aaron Henry and Charles Evers.

The first organizational alternative to the Freedom Democratic party was the Mississippi Democratic Council (MDC), formed early in the summer of 1965. Spearheading this effort was Claude Ramsay, state president of the AFL-CIO. Labor organizers in Mississippi were about as unpopular as civil rights workers, and while sympathetic to the goals of the movement, Ramsey had kept a low profile during the early 1960s, in part because the rank and file of the labor movement were strongly segregationist. But in mid-July, 1965, approximately 125 people responded to his call to build "a Loyalist Mississippi Democratic group to restore relations with the national party." Nearly three-fourths of those attending the founding meeting were white, including Hodding Carter III, editor of the *Delta Democrat-Times*. Of the black Mississippians, most prominent were Charles Evers, Aaron Henry, and Charles Young, a prosperous Meridian businessman. No one connected with SNCC, CORE, or FDP was invited to this meeting.[36]

The MDC all but died aborning. Lyndon Johnson was still unwilling to offend powerful Mississippians on Capitol Hill, such as Senators Eastland and Stennis, and did not offer support. Movement activists in Mississippi were outraged at this apparent effort to undermine their credibility, and only a handful of blacks continued to identify with MDC. After several meetings the organization dissolved. By this time, however, the moderates had found a viable alternative in the Mississippi Young Democrats.

The battle over the charter of the Young Democrats was fought between forces representing the MFDP and the new NAACP–labor–white moderate coalition. COFO activists had attempted to gain the YD charter at the Atlantic City convention but were rejected, ostensibly because of "technical failures in their application." (The Mississippi Young Democrats had ceased to function even before the 1964 election campaign.) Early in 1965 a small group of Delta whites, led by Hodding Carter III and attorney Doug Wynn (one of the four "regular" delegates who did not walk out in Atlantic City), began to reorganize existing YD clubs, particularly on white college campuses. Allied once again with the state NAACP leadership, they prepared to do battle with FDP at a state Young Democrats convention, called to adopt a new constitution and to elect officers. Representatives of the Carter and FDP factions met prior to the convention, held at the Heidelberg Hotel in Jackson, to lay out ground rules. They agreed that Gordon Henderson, a political science professor at Millsaps College, would be the chair and that no elections would take place before the afternoon. (Students at Tougaloo and Millsaps colleges had summer school classes in the morning, and a number of blacks from out-of-town would also be arriving late.)

Yet when the convention opened, it was apparent that the NAACP-Carter people, in a majority at the morning session, had a separate agenda. Ignoring the earlier agreements, they elected their own convention chair, black NAACP youth leader Johnny Frazier, and proceeded with the election of officers, choosing Hodding Carter and Cleveland Donald (one of a handful of black students enrolled at Ole Miss) as YD cochairs and filling other offices with anti-FDP delegates. By the afternoon session, however, FDP supporters comprised a strong majority at the convention and proceeded to censure and remove Frazier as convention chair by a vote of 175–114. At this point Hodding Carter called on all "true" Young Democrats to follow him downstairs to a room reserved earlier, where they would hold a "true Young Democratic state convention." About 30 percent of the delegates walked out with Carter, and the two factions met separately for the rest of the afternoon. This angry confrontation further exacerbated the bitter divisions. Eventually, the national Young Democrats (who shared their parent organizations's distrust of the MFDP) recognized the Carter-NAACP group as its legitimate Mississippi representative.[37]

All this might appear to be much ado about very little. Nationally, the Young Democrats were not a powerful group, even within the party, for the organization was mostly a training ground for young politicians. But for the new white-black coalition, capturing the young Democrats' charter was extremely important. Whites like Wynn and Carter had no previous civil rights credentials, and the NAACP in Mississippi had for years been in the shadow of the young SNCC and CORE activists and their grass-roots allies. Operating under the Young Democrats' banner gave this group visibility and an organizational base from which to operate. Looking back on these developments, Doug Wynn, who became the Young Democrats' legal counsel, observed that obtaining the state YD charter was essential to the later success of his faction.[38]

For the next three years both the MFDP and the Mississippi Young Democrats sought recognition from the national Democratic party as the heir apparent to the segregationist regulars, who gave no indication of opening their party to meaningful black participation. But a more important issue was at stake: would the Mississippi movement continue to be an independent, grass-roots struggle led by representatives of the dispossessed? Or would the displaced black middle class, assisted by its new white allies, reassert its control and direct the movement into the political mainstream, subject to the dictates of the national party? Built on the foundation laid by COFO, the FDP enjoyed widespread support at the local level. Its challengers were a faction in search of a party. Yet the contest would not be fought on a level playing field. Cautiously at first, the administration of Lyndon Johnson intervened to assist the middle-class moderate alternative to FDP militancy. Working through the president's friend, Doug Wynn, the White House staff privately encouraged the moderates, while keeping FDP at arm's length. But the administration provided more than moral support, employing the politics of poverty to bolster the position of the middle-class faction.[39]

A product of the Great Society's War on Poverty, the Child Development Group of Mississippi (CDGM) was one of the nation's pioneer Head Start programs. Launched in the summer of 1965, CDGM provided poor children with preschool training, medical care, and two nutritious meals a day. It also offered employment at a living wage to hundreds of local people serving as paraprofessionals and teachers at the Head Start centers. By the following summer CDGM was serving more than twelve thousand children in 121 preschools in twenty-eight counties. The Office of Economic Opportunity cited it as a model program, praising CDGM for its parent involvement and creative use of subprofessionals. Robert Coles testified: "In ten years of work in child psychiatry I have yet to see a program like this one. Against almost impossible odds children have been taught and also receive the benefits of medical care in a manner and with a thoroughness that is truly extraordinary." Yet in the fall of 1966, OEO abruptly terminated CDGM, having hastily and secretly recruited another group of Mississippians to apply for a Head Start charter under the name of Mississippi Action for Progress (MAP).[40]

The story of the demise of CDGM is far too complex to rehearse here except in its barest outline. Essentially what transpired is that while white elected officials in Mississippi initially would have no part of this program, by the end of the summer of 1965 they were dismayed to see that CDGM was succeeding not only as an educational institution, but that it was also taking seriously what OEO director Sargent Shriver had said about "maximum participation of the poor in the solutions of their own problems." The professional directors of CDGM had not been civil rights workers, but drew upon the organizing talents of a number of movement veterans to develop a community action program that supported the work of the Freedom Democratic party. In a broad but real sense, then, for the first time civil rights forces had political patronage to dispense, and federally funded patronage at that. All this was too much for John Stennis, who took to the Senate floor to accuse CDGM of crimes ranging from fiscal mismanagement to providing bail for its employees arrested in demonstrations. Other important officials joined in the attack, and their pressure resulted in Shriver's abandonment of a Head Start program once considered "the best in the country."[41]

The OEO decision to replace CDGM with MAP had political implications beyond the question of who would run Head Start. MAP's charter went to three white men: Owen Cooper, a Yazoo City industrialist; LeRoy Percy, a wealthy Delta planter; and Hodding Carter III. Its appointed governing board of twelve men included Aaron Henry and Charles Young, who with Carter were the organizers of the ill-fated Mississippi Democratic Conference and its successor, the Mississippi Young Democrats. That the original MAP board was all-male is not coincidental. Women should work with the children in their local programs, nurturing ideas of individual freedom. Questions involving money and power, on the other hand, were men's business. The same held true in the political arena. When one thinks of MFDP the names that come quickly to mind are Fannie Lou Hamer, Annie Devine, and Victoria Gray. Women were the dominant group in the Freedom party. Among the challengers, the leading spokespersons were Aaron Henry, Charles Evers, and Hodding Carter. Class, race, *and* gender were at the heart of the internal battles waged in the post-1965 period over the control of the poverty program and national political recognition.[42]

Loss of the poverty program was a serious blow to community organizers in Mississippi, especially those active in the Freedom Democratic party. Control over millions of federal dollars flowing into the state gave the moderate faction headed by Carter and Henry the legitimacy—and patronage—it needed. FDP was now broke and under heavy attack for its increasing radicalism, as Black Power and the escalating war in Vietnam moved the party further away from the Democratic mainstream.

In late July of 1965, at the time when organized labor and NAACP officers were setting up the Mississippi Democratic Council, a black McComb resident named John Shaw was killed while serving in Vietnam. Shaw had been active in the McComb movement four years earlier, when SNCC first moved into the state. Enraged that a man who could not find freedom at home had lost his life on a foreign battlefield, two McComb activists, Clint Hopson and Joe Martin, circulated a leaflet throughout the community and sent a copy to Jackson, where it was published in the MFDP *Newsletter*, the organization's official publication. The McComb statement listed "five reasons why Negroes should not be in any war fighting for America," bluntly asserting that "Negro boys should not honor the draft here in Mississippi. Mothers should encourage their sons not to go." Although the *Newsletter* printed the statement without endorsement, FDP opponents inside and outside the state seized upon the document to portray the Freedom party as unpatriotic and extremist.

Denunciations from the white Mississippi establishment were to be expected, but what damaged FDP most was the criticism from blacks. The NAACP's Charles Evers said that "for Negro citizens to ignore the draft can only serve to destroy that which they have fought so hard to achieve." R. Jess Brown, a black Jackson attorney and movement supporter, took issue with the McComb statement, declaring that blacks needed to "fight on a battlefield" as part of the struggle to win freedom at home. And Charles Diggs, the black congressional representative from Detroit, blasted the statement as "ridiculous and completely irresponsible."[43]

The FDP leadership moved quickly to attempt to control the damage. Lawrence Guyot, chair of the FDP executive committee, and committee member Ed King issued a statement pointing out that the leaflet did not represent the policy of the MFDP, and Guyot later told the *New York Times* that if drafted, he would serve in the armed forces. But both men upheld "the right of our members to discuss and act upon all issues" and argued that it was "very easy to understand why Negro citizens of McComb, themselves the victims of bombings, Klan-inspired terrorism, and harassment arrests, should resent the death of a citizen of McComb while fighting in Viet Nam for 'freedom' not enjoyed by the Negro community of McComb."[44]

The McComb antiwar leaflet was one of the first broadsides calling on young men to refuse to fight, a position that would gain widespread acceptance among activists as the conflict in Southeast Asia intensified. But in the short run the Freedom Democratic party lost credibility at a time when it was most vulnerable to challenge by the "respectable" moderate coalition of Mississippi blacks and whites, who pledged allegiance to Lyndon Johnson's Vietnam policy and who exploited the McComb statement to their political advantage. The AFL-CIO's Claude Ramsey went so far as to equate the FDP with the Ku Klux Klan and expressed the conviction that the "great majority of Mississippi Negroes . . . will continue to follow the responsible Negro leadership of this state in lieu of the anarchists in their midst today."[45]

That "responsible Negro leadership" had benefited from the flap over Vietnam, the failure of the FDP congressional challenge, the decision to fund MAP instead of CDGM, and from support by important liberal Democrats in Washington. Moreover, passage of the 1965 Voting Rights Act worked more to the advantage of the NAACP-led faction than to that of the Freedom Democrats. Although white resistance to black registration and voting continued in many areas of the state, the presence of federal registrars in problem counties soon made a dramatic difference. Now that registering to vote no longer carried with it grave risks, middle-class school teachers, entrepreneurs, and ministers got their names on the books and sought positions of political leadership in their communities. Enforcement of the voting rights act also made possible the meteoric rise of Charles Evers.

Evers became the subject of controversy the moment he returned to Mississippi in the summer of 1963, when he announced shortly after his brother Medgar's funeral that he would assume the position of

NAACP state field secretary. For the previous seven years Charles had lived in Chicago, where by his own admission he had been a bootlegger, numbers runner, and petty thief, as well as a teacher and tavern owner. Back in Mississippi, Evers cultivated the image of the maverick. Constantly at odds with his NAACP superiors in New York (who did not want to offer him the position of field secretary to begin with), he refused to cooperate with the COFO leadership and tried to undermine its programs. Yet early in 1965 Evers began to develop a power base in southwest Mississippi and, with the implementation of the voting rights act, registered thousands of black voters.

Where COFO and the FDP had avoided the cult of the personality and fostered indigenous leadership, Evers was an old-fashioned political boss, whipping his troops into line, commanding their loyalty through the power of his personality. A charismatic figure, Evers combined flamboyant behavior with a down-home approach. He spoke the language of the people, and, like Sen. Joseph McCarthy, another successful demagogue, Evers appeared to revel in his reputation as an unsavory character. The national NAACP office could not control him; the Young Democrats kept him at arm's length; and the FDP looked on in dismay as he emerged as the most powerful black politician in the state. Eventually, all of these organizations would have to accept Charles Evers on his terms.[46]

Evers's political clout became apparent in the early summer of 1966, when the Freedom Democratic party fielded a slate of candidates to run against the white incumbents in the congressional primary elections. Short of staff and funds, the FDP candidates fared poorly, except in those counties controlled by Evers. in Claiborne and Jefferson counties, for example, the FDP senatorial candidate, Rev. Clifton R. Whitley, defeated incumbent James O. Eastland. But in the general election, Evers put out the word that he was supporting Eastland's Republican opponent instead of Whitley, now running as an independent. The results were dramatic: where Whitley had polled 1,639 votes in the Claiborne County primary with Evers's support, he received only 120 votes in the general election; and in Jefferson, his 1,725 primary total fell to 69 votes in November.[47] FDP leaders were disappointed with the party's performance in the congressional elections and dismayed that black voters in the southwest were apparently securely in Evers's pocket. But the 1966 elections were to be overshadowed by a much more newsworthy event—the Meredith March—which gave birth to the Black Power battle cry.

When on June 5, 1966, James Meredith set out alone to walk the 220 miles from Memphis to Jackson, his stated purpose was to persuade Mississippi blacks that times had changed and that it was safe for them to register and vote. On the second day of his trip Meredith was shot and wounded by a sniper alongside the road, just inside the Mississippi border. The subsequent decision by all the major civil rights organizations to continue Meredith's journey led to the last great march of the civil rights years, one that from the outset was steeped in controversy. In Greenwood, Stokely Carmichael stirred the crowd with his call for Black Power, and Americans became aware of the nationalist sentiment that had been building within the movement for two years. The Meredith March once again propelled SNCC into the limelight and revealed the declining influence of Martin Luther King with militant activists. It also brought to the surface the growing antiwhite feelings among black activists and marked the beginning of the end of white participation in SNCC and CORE.[48]

Ironically, the march through Mississippi had a greater impact nationally than locally, where it served mainly to deepen the divisions between moderates and militants in the black community. Guyot and other FDP leaders helped plan and organize the march and registered approximately four thousand new voters. But it was Stokely Carmichael and Martin Luther King, not the Freedom Democrats, who commanded media attention, and the march did little to increase traditional political activity across the state. Some FDP activists, frustrated over the lack of progress on the political front, drew inspiration from the march to push FDP to embrace a Black Power agenda, one that would minimize or eliminate the participation of whites in the organization, and abandon the goal of achieving recognition by the national Democratic party. Yet while the party's rhetoric grew more strident over the next eighteen months, Guyot and the FDP executive committee continued to steer a middle course, alienating FDP from both SNCC radicals and NAACP stalwarts. Until the end, the Freedom party remained open to white participation; of the fifty to sixty women and men actively engaged in community organization in 1966–67, a substantial minority were whites, and FDP drew much support from the Delta Ministry, an organization supported by the National

Council of Churches that had begun operations in Mississippi in the fall of 1964.[49]

Mississippi held state and local elections in 1967, with both the NAACP-led coalition and the Freedom Democratic party fielding candidates for county and municipal positions ranging from justice of the peace to county sheriff. Nearly 200,000 blacks were now registered in Mississippi, and blacks constituted a voting majority in several localities. These numbers did not automatically translate into victories, as FDP learned in a special election held in the town of Sunflower, in Sen. James Eastland's home county. Finding widespread evidence of discrimination against potential black voters, the federal courts had declared the 1965 Sunflower elections unconstitutional and had called a new election for May, 1967. Although black voters outnumbered whites 185–154, whites won all of the races in the special election. Threats and economic intimidation played a role in the defeat, but disunity in the black community was also a factor. Joseph Harris, campaign manager for Sunflower, later sadly observed, "Our people did not stick together." Faced with a black majority, white candidates for the first time solicited black votes, with apparent success. FDP's selection of candidates may also have been a factor. For example, more conservative black voters were not comfortable with the party's decision to run Otis Brown, Jr., a twenty-one-year-old former SNCC worker, for mayor. Although a majority of those voting were black, Brown lost his race to the white incumbent by 120–191.[50] Such would not be the case in Holmes County, where a middle-class schoolteacher, Robert Clark, became the first African American to sit in the Mississippi legislature in this century.

Clark's election represented the high point of the Freedom Democratic party's 1967 campaign. The Holmes County movement was unique. From the beginning it had been led by a group of land-owning black farmers who, with the help of SNCC workers and white volunteers, had organized the county's black majority into an effective political force. As a teacher, Clark was well known throughout the county, and his credentials served him well with members of the small black middle class. Clark's white opponent did not campaign for the black vote, and although there were irregularities on election day, a massive black turnout ensured Clark's narrow victory. Holmes County was a showcase of black organization and dedication, but in other counties the 1967 election results were mixed. Of the twenty-five candidates supported by the NAACP, eleven were elected, the majority in the southwestern counties organized by Charles Evers. The FDP ran sixty candidates, most as independents running in Delta counties, and only six won election.[51]

The most interesting political development that year was the agreement that the two factions, the NAACP-led coalition and the FDP, would put their political differences aside and support all black candidates running for office. A statement released by Guyot and other FDP leaders noted that "although statewide unity in any organizational or formal fashion has not been achieved, there exists an informal and unarticulated agreement among the differing political camps within the Black community to coexist throughout the election year." Both sides realized that the common enemy was white supremacy and continued infighting among blacks would be counterproductive, if not suicidal. For the Freedom Democrats, it was now apparent that the party was at a crossroads. Funding had dried up, political support from outside the state had diminished, and, despite the Clark victory, the party had little to show for its efforts during the 1967 election year. The NAACP and the Young Democrats, on the other hand, hoped to win recognition at the 1968 Democratic national convention but realized that without the endorsement of the FDP people who had captured the nation's attention four years earlier in Atlantic City, their own efforts would lack legitimacy. Throughout the winter of 1967–68, both factions began to explore the possibility of sending a united delegation to the 1968 convention to challenge the Mississippi segregationists. They took a major step toward this goal when Charles Evers, running for Congress in a special election, announced that the FDP's chair, Lawrence Guyot, would serve as his campaign chairman, with FDP national committeeman Ed King as his coordinator for speaking engagements. Evers lost the race in a runoff, but that he received the endorsement of his bitter rivals was a remarkable turn of events.[52]

The decision of FDP leaders to come to terms with their opponents and to mount another convention challenge did not sit well with many of the party's rank-and-file members. When in September, 1967, the FDP executive committee announced that the party would challenge the regulars in 1968, dissidents spoke out against the move, recalling the failure of the 1964 challenge and maintaining that FDP should work independently to build strong institutions in the black community. But when it became apparent that the NAACP and the Young Democrats were organizing their own challenging delegation, Guyot let it be known that FDP would be willing to unite with the moderates "in this political confrontation against Eastland's party." In late June the "loyalist" coalition took shape, composed of the state NAACP, the Prince Hall Masons, the Young Democrats, the (black) Mississippi Teachers Association, representatives from the labor movement, and the Freedom Democratic party.[53]

It was, on the surface, an unlikely alliance. Fannie Lou Hamer observed, "These same folks in 1964 were willing to sell us down the drain and tried to do it." Hodding Carter, leader of the Young Democrats, had in the past used the editorial columns of the *Delta Democrat Times* to excoriate the FDP, charging that its ranks were infiltrated by communists. And despite the decision to support Charles Evers in his congressional race, activists had not forgotten Evers riding roughshod over FDP in earlier organizational campaigns in southwestern Mississippi. Still, FDP was not in a position to mount a serious challenge of its own, and the alternative was to stay at home and have no impact on the convention proceedings. Scorning what he called "nothing but rhetoric on the left [where] you have a lot of radical theory and little work is being done," Lawrence Guyot defended the decision to join the coalition: "This challenge is indigenous, issue oriented, and broad-based. This is a mass challenge and the people support it."[54]

On August 11, 1968, the "loyalists" held their state convention at the Masonic Temple in Jackson, the scene of the FDP convention four years earlier. In contrast to that earlier gathering, the 1968 audience "seemed more affluent and content."[55] The moderate faction was in control of the convention, with Aaron Henry as chair. Selection of the remaining delegates was a cut-and-dried affair. FDP's earlier insistence that it be allotted half the delegates gave way to reality, and the party ultimately agreed to accept ten of the forty-four convention seats. An at-large slate of delegates had been chosen in advance, agreed to by representatives of the six groups in the coalition. Thus FDP delegates not privy to that meeting were dismayed when nominations of FDP members from the floor did not draw support from its own party leadership. The nominating committee had also agreed to support Rep. Robert Clark as the Loyalists' male representative to the Democratic

National Committee, but here Charles Evers engineered the convention's only surprise. Evers had finished second to Clark in the earlier vote, but when the NAACP leader was nominated from the floor an orchestrated demonstration broke out, with confetti falling from the balcony and a rock and roll band playing near the stage. FDP delegate John Buffington remembered that when he rose to speak on the nomination, "One guy asked if I was for Charles Evers. I said 'No,' and the mike was cut off. I tried to speak and was pulled from the stage and my jacket was ripped." Evers won the vote by a landslide. One convention observer commented, "That's as close to a machine as you can get."[56]

That the Loyalist delegation would be seated at the stormy Democratic National Convention in Chicago was a foregone conclusion. The white regulars had permitted only minimal black participation in the selection of delegates, and most whites were committed to the independent candidacy of Alabama governor George Wallace. All of the three major contenders for the presidential nomination—Hubert Humphrey, Eugene McCarthy, and George McGovern—had endorsed the Loyalist challenge well in advance of the convention. When the final votes were tallied, the national media trumpeted the victory as a triumph for the civil rights forces in Mississippi, and in a sense it was. But a different breed had captured the movement banner: urban, educated, and affluent, these new leaders had their own agenda. Few of them were organizers, and they had little contact with the black masses, for whom they professed to speak. The 1968 convention was in effect the swan song of the Mississippi Freedom Democratic party. It continued to function in areas such as Holmes County, where it had been strong. But attempts at reorganizing the party on the state level failed. Some FDP activists decided to work with the Loyalists, now the "official" Democratic party of Mississippi. Others, including FDP chair Lawrence Guyot, soon left the state.[57]

In 1992, more than two decades after the tumultuous events of the 1960s, the legacy of the Freedom Democratic party, and the SNCC and CORE activists who brought it into being, is visible across the face of Mississippi. Nearly two dozen African Americans are now in the state legislature; hundreds of blacks hold elective office on the local and county level. Most dramatic, a black man named Mike Espy is a member of the United States Congress, representing the Delta district that had been the scene of so much movement activity — and brutal white repression. Middle-class blacks have made tremendous strides since the 1960s, and the Jim Crow signs have long since disappeared. Perhaps the most revealing symbol of the new Mississippi is that the Jackson *Clarion-Ledger*, once the champion of white supremacy, led the battle to reopen the trial of Byron de la Beckwith, the man accused of the murder of Medgar Evers.

And yet for most black Mississippians the present resembles too much the past. Poverty is endemic; educational and economic opportunities are limited; racism and its effects remain visible in every community in the state. Ironically, the men and women who made the movement of the 1960s — sharecroppers, maids, small farmers, and workers — have benefited least from the changes taking place over the past two decades. The vision of Fannie Lou Hamer, one of political and economic democracy, remains just that — another dream deferred. The proud history of the black struggle in Mississippi and throughout the South, the courage and humanity of thousands of people working to take charge of their destiny, tells us much about the possibilities for achieving racial justice in America. It is also a potent reminder of the distance yet to be traveled.

NOTES

1. Mississippi *Constitution*, 1890, Article 12, Sections pp. 240–43, 256; Neil R. McMillen, *Dark Journey: Black Mississippians in the Age of Jim Crow* (Urbana: University of Illinois Press, 1989), pp. 42–43; Jackson *Daily News*, June 23, 1946; U.S. Senate, 79th Cong., 2nd sess., *Hearings before the Special Committee to Investigate Senatorial Campaign Expenditures*, 1946 (Washington, D.C.: U.S. Government Printing Office, 1947), 88–90, 19.

2. U.S. Commission on Civil Rights, *With Liberty and Justice for All* (Washington, D.C.: U.S. Government Printing Office, 1959), pp. 50–51; John Barlow Martin, *The Deep South Says Never* (New York: Ballantine Books, 1957), pp. 28–29; Reed Sarrat, *The Ordeal of Desegregation* (New York: Harper & Row, 1966), p. 302; New York *Post*, Nov. 30, 1955; *Delta Democrat Times*, Aug. 18, 1955; NAACP press release, Aug. 18, 1955, and "Are You Curious about Mississippi," undated NAACP press release, both in Papers of the National Association for the Advancement of Colored People, Library of Congress; the definitive book on the Citizens' Council is Neil R. McMillen, *The Citizens' Council: Organized Resistance to the Second Reconstruction, 1954–64* (Urbana: University of Illinois Press, 1971). On Medgar Evers, see Mrs. Medgar [Myrlie] Evers, with William Peters, *For Us, the Living* (New York: Ace Paperback Edition, 1970).

3. Quoted in David Halberstam, "Tallahatchie County Acquits a Peckerhead," *Reporter*, Apr. 19, 1956, p. 28; "Statistical Report of Medgar Evers for Year 1959, January 1–December 5," NAACP prs.

4. John Dittmer, "The Politics of the Mississippi Movement, 1954–1964," in Charles Eagles, ed., *The Civil Rights Movement in America* (Jackson: University Press of Mississippi, 1986), pp. 72–73.

5. Ibid., p. 74; Clayborne Carson, *In Struggle: SNCC and the Black Awakening of the 1960s* (Cambridge: Harvard University Press, 1981), p. 78.

6. Neil R. McMillen, "Black Enfranchisement in Mississippi: Federal Enforcement and Black Protest in the 1960s," *Journal of Southern History* 43 (Aug., 1977): 356; interview with Burke Marshall, Dec. 3, 1983, New Haven, Conn.

7. Howard Zinn, *SNCC: The New Abolitionists* (Boston: Beacon Press, 1965), pp. 99–101; Carson, *In Struggle*, pp. 97–98.

8. Len Holt, *The Summer That Didn't End* (London: Heinemann, 1966), p. 158; unsigned letter, Aug. 6, 1964, in Elizabeth Sutherland, ed., *Letters from Mississippi* (New York: McGraw Hill, 1965), pp. 213–14; Paul Good, *The Trouble I've Seen: White Journalist/Black Movement* (Washington, D.C.: Howard University Press, 1975), p. 170.

9. Good, *Trouble I've Seen*, p. 172.

10. Interview with Robert Moses, Aug. 15, 1983, Cambridge, Mass.; Paul Cowan, *The Making of an Un-American: A Dialogue with Experience* (New York: Viking Press, 1970), pp. 40–43; Memorandum, Casey Hayden to Jackson FDP, "Notes on Conversation with Al Lowenstein," July 14, 1964, copy in Jan Hillegas Private Collection, Jackson, Miss.; Ed King, interviewed by Anne Romaine, 1965, Highlander Center, Tenn., pp. 1–10, Anne Romaine Papers, State Historical Society of Wisconsin [SHSW], Madison, Wis.

11. Mary King, *Freedom Song: A Personal Story of the 1960s Civil Rights Movement* (New York: William Morrow, 1987), p. 343; James Forman, *The Making of Black Revolutionaries* (New York: Macmillan, 1975; Open Hand paperback edition, 1985), p. 387; Jackson *Daily News*, Aug. 13, 1964; Holt, *Summer That Didn't End*, p. 165; *New York Times*, Aug. 22, 1964.

12. Joseph Rauh, interviewed by Anne Romaine, June 16, 1965, Washington, D.C., Romaine Papers; *New York Times*, Aug. 23, 1964.

13. "Partial Proceedings of the Democratic National Convention, 1964, Credentials Committee, Aug. 22, 1964," pp. 43–44, Joseph Rauh Papers, SHSW; *New York Times*, Aug. 23, 1964; Carson, *In Struggle*, p. 125.

14. Lyndon Johnson, *The Vantage Point: Perspectives of the Presidency, 1963–69* (New York: Holt, Rhinehart and Winston, 1971), p. 101; Godfrey Hodgson, *America in Our Time: From World War II to Nixon, What Happened and Why* (New York, Vintage, 1978), pp. 213–14; Memorandum, Jack Valenti to President Johnson, July 20, 1964, and Karl Rolvaag to Walter Jenkins, July 27, 1964, both in White House Central File [WHCF], Lyndon Baines Johnson Library [LBJ], Austin, Tex.; Joseph Rauh, interviewed by Paige Mulholland, Aug. 1, 1969, Washington, D.C., pp. 13–14, and President's Diary and Diary Backup, Aug. 15–26, 1964, both in Oral History, LBJ.

15. *Intelligence Activities and the Rights of Americans, Book II, Final Report of the Select Committee to Study Governmental Operations, United States Senate* (Washington, D.C.: U.S. Government Printing Office, 1976), p. 117.

16. Kenneth O'Reilly, *Racial Matters: The FBI's Secret File on Black America, 1960–1972* (New York: Free Press, 1989), pp. 186–88; C. D. DeLoach to "Dear Bishop," Sept. 10, 1964, WHCF, Name File, LBJ; Diary and Diary Backup, Aug. 20–27, 1964, LBJ.

17. David J. Garrow, *Bearing the Cross: Martin Luther King, Jr., and the Southern Christian Leadership Conference* (New York: William Morrow, 1986), p. 347.

18. *New York Times*, Aug. 26, 1964.

19. Edwin King, "'Speak Truth to Power': The Mississippi Freedom Democratic Party," unpublished manuscript, pp. 126, 185–86; Joseph Rauh, Remarks at "Freedom Summer Reviewed" conference, Tougaloo, Miss., Nov. 1, 1974, pp. 35–36 (transcript in author's possession).

20. *New York Times*, Aug. 26, 1964; Theodore White, *The Making of the President, 1964* (New York: Atheneum), p. 335. Hubert Humphrey described his assignment in working out the compromise as "aggravating." Had he failed, would Johnson have chosen someone else as his vice-presidential nominee? "It is a question I have never been able to answer" (Hubert Humphrey, *The Education of a Public Man: My Life and Politics* [New York: Doubleday, 1976], pp. 299–300).

21. Moses interview; Fannie Lou Hamer, interviewed by Robert Wright, 1968, Ruleville, Miss., Howard Civil Rights Documentation Project [CRDP], p. 29, Howard University Archives; Henry Sias, interviewed by Robert Wright, 1968, Issaquena County, Miss., Howard CRDP, p. 20; Fannie Lou Hamer, interviewed by Anne and Howard Romaine, 1965, Highlander Center, p. 12, Romaine Papers; Carson, *In Struggle*, p. 126.

22. Interview with Joyce Ladner, May 9, 1985, Washington, D.C.; Bob Moses, interview with Clayborne Carson, March 29, 1982, Cambridge, Mass., p. 38; Cleveland Sellers, with Robert Terrell, *The River of No Return: The Autobiography of a Black Militant and the Life and Death of SNCC* (New York: William Morrow, 1973), p. 111.

23. Aaron Henry to President Lyndon B. Johnson, Aug. 30, 1964, Name File, LBJ; FDP, "The Convention Challenge," undated [fall, 1964], Robert Stone Papers (in the author's possession); Julius Lester, *Look Out, Whitey! Black Power's Gon' Get Your Mama* (New York: Dial Press, 1968), p. 28; Forman, *Black Revolutionaries*, p. 423.

24. Although chair of the Freedom Democratic Party, Guyot was not at the Atlantic City convention; he was serving a sentence in the Hattiesburg jail during convention week.

25. Lawrence Guyot, interviewed by Anne and Howard Romaine, 1965, Highlander Center, p. 21, Romaine Papers; *Southern Patriot*, Nov., 1966; Leslie Burl McLemore, "The Mississippi Freedom Democratic Party: A Case Study of Grass-Roots Politics," Ph.D. diss., University of Massachusetts, 1971, pp. 176–77. Written by a scholar-activist who was close to the events he describes, this dissertation contains a wealth of valuable information.

26. Robert Coles, "Social Struggles and Weariness," *Psychiatry* 27 (1964): 315, 308.

27. Minutes, "Canton–Valley View Staff Meeting," Dec. 3, 4, 1964, Joann Ooiman Robinson Papers, SHSW.

28. Moses interview; interview with David Dennis, July 12, 1983, Lafayette, La.; Carson, *In Struggle*, pp. 170–74.

29. Morton Stavis, "A Century of Struggle for Black Enfranchisement in Mississippi: From the Civil War to the Congressional Challenge of 1965—And Beyond," *Mississippi Law Journal*, 57 (1987): 640–45; Lawrence Guyot and Michael Thelwell, "Toward Independent Political Power," *Freedomways* 6 (Third Quarter, 1966): 246–47; *New York Times*, Jan. 5, 1965. See also McLemore, "The Mississippi Freedom Democratic Party," chap. 4.

30. Stavis, "Century of Struggle," pp. 647–48, 660–64; Guyot and Thelwell, "To-

ward Independent Political Power," pp. 248–49. In regard to the position of the Johnson administration on the challenge, Drew Pearson reported that House Speaker Carl Albert told Representative Ryan that "the full weight of the Johnson Administration leadership would be thrown against him in favor of the Mississippians" (*Washington Post*, Jan. 8, 1965).

31. Memorandum to: Presidents of Branches, Youth Councils, College Chapters and State Conferences, from: John Morsell, Assistant Executive Director, re: Challenge to Mississippi Congressmen, March 22, 1965, NAACP Papers; Leon Shull, National Director, ADA, to National Officers, National Board, Chapter Chairmen, Dec. 19, 1964, and Memorandum from Lawrence Guyot to All Staff and FDP County Chairmen, Dec. 24, 1964, copies of both in the papers of the Student Nonviolent Coordinating Committee, reel 63; Stavis, "Century of Struggle," 658.

32. Memorandum to: Leon Shull, From: Curtis B. Gans, Re: Atlanta Trip and Other Matters, Nov. 20, 1964, Americans for Democratic Action Papers, unprocessed collection, State Historical Society of Wisconsin. I am indebted to Steven M. Gillon for supplying me with a copy of this document. See also Gillon's *Politics and Vision: The ADA and American Liberalism, 1947–1985* (New York: Oxford University Press, 1987), pp. 161–63; Rowland Evans and Robert Novak, "Inside Report: Civil Rights—Danger Ahead," New York *Herald Tribune*, Dec. 2, 1964, clipping in Edwin King Papers, Tougaloo College, Tougaloo, Miss.

33. Moses interview; Gloster Current to Bishop Steven G. Spottswood, and Members of the Board, Re: NAACP Withdrawal from COFO, Dec. 29, 1964, NAACP Papers; Ed King, interviewed by Anne Romaine, p. 10, Romaine Papers.

34. Gloster Current to Charles Evers, July 17, 1964, NAACP Papers.

35. *Washington Post*, Dec. 31, 1964; Current to Spottswood . . . Dec. 29, 1964.

36. Mississippi Freedom Democratic Party *Newsletter*, July 28, 1965, SNCC Papers, reel 69; New York *Herald-Tribune*, Aug. 9, 1965, clipping in Ed King Papers; Rowland Evans and Robert Novak, "Inside Report: The Mississippi Moderates," New York *Herald-Tribune*, Aug. 9, 1965, clipping in Ed King Papers; William Simpson, "The Birth of the Mississippi 'Loyalist Democrats', (1965–1968)," *Journal of Mississippi History* 44 (Feb., 1982): 28–29.

37. R. Spencer Oliver to Mrs. Murnett Y. Washington, March 26, 1965, Hunter Morey Papers, SHSW; Ibid.; Elmer Cooper, untitled report on the Mississippi Young Democrats' Convention, Sept. 6, 1965, Wilson F. Minor, unedited news story for the New Orleans *Times-Picayune*, Wilson F. Minor Papers, Special Collections, Mitchell Memorial Library, Mississippi State University; McLemore, "The Mississippi Freedom Democratic Party," p. 414.

38. Interview with Douglas Wynn, Dec. 4, 1984, Greenville, Miss.

39. Dittmer, "Politics of the Mississippi Movement," pp. 166–67, n. 67.

40. *New York Times*, Oct. 19, 1966; Robert Coles quoted in Citizens' Crusade Against Poverty, Board of Inquiry, "Final Report on the Child Development Group of Mississippi," p. 6, undated copy in Martin Luther King Papers, Martin Luther King Center [MLK], Atlanta, Ga.; James Ridgeway, "Shriver Drops CDGM," *New Republic*, Oct. 15, 1966.

41. Office of Economic Opportunity, *Administrative History, Vol. I, Part* 1, pp. 66–70, LBJ; Jackson *Clarion-Ledger*, Aug. 23, 1966; *New York Times*, Mar. 7, 1966.

42. Jackson *Clarion-Ledger*, Sept. 30, 1966; MFDP, "What is MAP?" undated, Hillegas Collection; "Information on Mississippi Action for Progress: Who Are Their

Board Members? What Are Their Ties?" undated, unsigned copy in Tom Levin Papers, MLK.

43. MFDP *Newsletter*, July 28, 1965, SNCC Papers, reel 69; Joanne Grant, ed., *Black Protest: History, Documents, and Analyses, 1619 to the Present* (Greenwich, Conn.: Fawcett, 1968), pp. 415–16; McLemore, "Mississippi Freedom Democratic Party," pp. 234–38.

44. MFDP news release, "MFDP and Vietnam," July 31, 1965, Hillegas Collection; *New York Times*, Aug. 4, 1965.

45. Mississippi AFL-CIO news release, "Statement by: Claude Ramsey, President," Aug. 2, 1965, Eugene Cox Papers, Box 1, Mitchell Library, Mississippi State University.

46. Charles Evers and Grace Halsell, *Evers* (New York: World Publishing Company, 1971), pp. 96–106, 113; Gloster Current to Roy Wilkins, "Memorandum Re: Charles Evers," Sept. 9, 1963, and Current to Evers, Aug. 21, 1963, both in NAACP Papers; "Report on a Meeting of Community Organizers in Mississippi," Oct. 29, 1966, Hillegas Collection.

47. McLemore, "Mississippi Freedom Democratic Party," p. 314; "Official Vote Tabulation, State of Mississippi—Regular Election, November 8, 1966, for Senator to the 90th U.S. Congress by Counties," quoted in McLemore, ibid., 335; "Report on a Meeting of Community Organizers."

48. Steven F. Lawson, *In Pursuit of Power: Southern Blacks and Electoral Politics, 1965–1982* (New York: Columbia University Press, 1985), pp. 52–62; Carson, *In Struggle*, pp. 207–11.

49. Lawson, *In Pursuit of Power*, 62; Fannie Lou Hamer to Amzie [Moore], Oct. 24, 1966, Amzie Moore Papers, SHSW.

50. *New York Times*, May 3, 1967; *Southern Patriot*, April, May, 1967; Sandra Nystrom and Eleanor Holmes Norton, "Times Changing in Sunflower," clipping in Anne and Carl Braden Papers, SHSW; *New America*, June 18, 1967; McLemore, "Mississippi Freedom Democratic Party," pp. 343–76; Lawson, *In Pursuit of Power*, pp. 99–102.

51. Lawson, *In Pursuit of Power*, p. 99; McLemore, "Mississippi Freedom Democratic Party," pp. 377–88.

52. "Mississippians to Elect Negro Candidates to 'Dear Friend,'" undated [1967], Amzie Moore Papers; McLemore, *In Pursuit of Power*, p. 396.

53. Freedom Information Service, *Mississippi Newsletter*, Sept. 22, 1967, Hillegas Collection; McLemore, "Mississippi Freedom Democratic Party," pp. 420–21.

54. *Southern Patriot*, Nov., Sept., 1968.

55. McLemore, "Mississippi Freedom Democratic Party," p. 452.

56. Freedom Information Service, *Mississippi Newletter*, Aug. 16, 1968; *Southern Patriot*, Nov., 1968; McLemore, "Mississippi Freedom Democratic Party," p. 441.

57. Dittmer, "Politics of the Mississippi Movement," p. 92; Ibid., McLemore, "Mississippi Freedom Democratic Party," pp. 456–57; Lawson, *In Pursuit of Power*, pp. 115–18.

GEORGE C. WRIGHT

The Civil Rights Movement in Kentucky, 1900–70*

ANY ASSESSMENT of the civil rights movement must take a long-term view. If we are to understand the events of the 1950s and 1960s, we must acknowledge the foundations laid by civil rights activists over the first half of the twentieth century. The central role of the NAACP in challenging Jim Crow through the courts is well-known; however, blacks throughout the South also campaigned at local levels to resist segregation. While these efforts were not successful, they reveal a core of strength that would later sustain the civil rights movement. A case study of the movement in Kentucky provides an excellent opportunity to trace the course of civil rights in this century.

Though already living in a segregated society, black Kentuckians in the early 1900s experienced new and even more restrictive Jim Crow practices that by the 1930s resulted in their exclusion from white society in virtually every way possible. At the turn of the century, a public library opened in Louisville. Blacks complained to city officials about their exclusion from the library, often noting with bitterness that as taxpayers, they should have the right to enter any public facility. Library officials eventually grew tired of their complaints and began working with black leaders to secure financial support from industrialist and philanthropist Andrew Carnegie to open two black libraries. Meanwhile, these officials continued prohibiting blacks from the library's main branch, a practice that remained in effect until 1950. The Henderson Public Library opened in 1904. Right from the start, the board of directors believed that allowing blacks access to the reading rooms and to borrow books "would totally destroy the usefulness of the Library to this community." To end black complaints, library officials moved a few books, which were "suited to the needs of the colored population," to the Eighth Street Colored School. Library officials viewed this dual system as an ideal arrangement: it would satisfy blacks by providing them with a library but, more importantly, as their report frankly stated, "it would leave the white population of the city undisturbed in their use of the Library building."[1]

Kentucky's black citizens were excluded from public hospitals even in life-threatening emergencies. In 1911, a black man was struck by a railroad train in Frankfort. Carried to the closest hospital, which was a white hospital, the man was refused admission because of his race. The man was then transported to the workhouse and left to die. On one occasion while responding to an alarm, several black firemen in Louisville were injured in a car collision. After being denied treatment at the public-supported Red Cross Hospital, they were taken to the all-black hospital. Unlike blacks in other Kentucky communities, Louisville blacks were fortunate even to have their own hospital. Even Lexington blacks did not have a hospital and usually received treatment and examinations by black physicians at a small "clinic."[2]

Integration probably existed in city parks throughout the nineteenth century with segregation occurring in the first two decades of the new century. In Henderson, for example, blacks and whites coexisted in Barret Park for years, but in 1903, white city officials and civic leaders called for limiting blacks to a specific area within the park. Hopkinsville instituted park segregation in the early 1900s by designating three playgrounds and two parks for whites, and one park for blacks. Racial integration existed in all of Lexington's parks until 1916. But in that year Frederick Douglass Park opened in the far west end of the city. Given its location, the park was practically inaccessible to all but the few blacks who lived in that immediate area. Nevertheless, this was the only park for blacks, though there were several playgrounds scattered throughout the city for them. For decades in the nineteenth century, whites and blacks in Louisville had shared the same parks, which usually had swimming pools, tennis courts, and baseball fields. Between 1910 and 1920, however, the city opened a few designated all-black parks. Blacks were still admitted to other parks, but they were prohibited from the swimming pools and tennis courts. Park segregation officially started in July, 1924, with the passing of a city ordinance. Despite the denouncement of the ordinance by Louisville blacks, it remained in place for thirty years.[3]

Beginning in the 1910s, whites in several Kentucky cities took steps to make certain that blacks remained excluded from white residential areas. In Henderson, a deed restriction written into a 1913 mortgage said "It is understood and agreed that the property above conveyed is not to be transferred by sale or lease to a person or persons of color." Madisonville, a city where blacks comprised 40 percent of the population, enacted a residential segregation ordinance in 1913.[4] Around 1910, a number of blacks began purchasing homes west of the downtown area in Louisville. Whites responded by passing the Louisville Residential Segregation Ordinance, which prohibited blacks from moving into designated all-white streets and whites from moving into all-black districts. After a three-year battle through the courts by the NAACP, the ordinance was overturned in November, 1917, by a unanimous decision of the United States Supreme Court. Yet the court's ruling did not lead to equal access to housing for Louisville blacks because they still confronted a number of obstacles — ranging from deed restrictions to overt violence — when they attempted to move to the westward areas of the city. Blacks were not able to move to Louisville's far-west end until the 1950s and 1960s.[5]

Blacks were clearly relegated to separate and inferior schools in Kentucky. The vast majority of Kentucky whites viewed black education as a burden, spending only the minimum required by law, if even that small amount. For decades, a succession of white educators maintained that the end product of black education should be the acceptance by blacks of "their place" in Southern society. As superintendent of education George Colvin explained to Robert W. Bingham, editor of the high influential Louisville *Courier-Journal*, in 1923, it was essential that the state's black citizens be educated in the South, not the North. He believed that education in the North tended to give blacks false ideas about their importance and make them discontent with their menial jobs in the South.[6]

The "right education" for blacks consisted primarily of industrial skills and only the basics in academic areas. Not surprisingly, in most areas of the state, whites refused to provide schools for blacks beyond eighth grade. There were only nine black public high schools in operation by the mid-1910s. This meant that the vast majority of Kentucky's black citizens either ended their schooling at the completion of the eighth grade or looked to small, private, religious schools to provide them with high school courses.

With whites unwilling to support black public education adequately, it should come as no surprise that the state's black institution of higher learning, Kentucky State College for Negroes, received funds only after allocations had been provided to white institutions of higher learning. Though labeled a college, Kentucky State was in reality a high school until the 1920s, with most of the students completing two years of high school courses. Because the school's mandate was to train teachers (tuition was free to any student pledged to teach in Kentucky), the normal department was the first course of study established at Kentucky State. The school also had agricultural, mechanical, and domestic departments—programs viewed as essential for the growth of Kentucky's black population.

Fortunately, in the early 1900s, Kentucky blacks were not limited to this state-supported college. They also matriculated at Berea College, a unique institution in the South. This private institution had been founded in 1855 by John Fee and Cassius Clay, and immediately after the Civil War, it started admitting black students. Moreover, Berea went far beyond tokenism in admitting blacks: by the 1880s, blacks comprised a little more than 60 percent of the student body. Also, James S. Hathaway, a black, served on the faculty. Considering the racism that dominated American society during the late-nineteenth century, Hathaway might have been the only black instructor in the nation teaching at a white college.[7]

To be sure, on occasion racial tension existed at the school, but Berea remained integrated even during the 1890s, when Pres. William G. Frost advocated a sharp reduction in the enrollment of black students. But the likelihood that Berea College could maintain its commitment to integrated education against the rising tide of racism, was very small indeed. In November, 1903, Carl Day, a state representative from Breathitt County, an area with only a handful of blacks, toured the Berea campus and expressed his outrage at the sight of blacks and whites "living together." In January, 1904, he introduced a bill, directed only at Berea, that imposed a one thousand dollar fine with one hundred dollars per day penalty upon any institution admitting both white and black students. The Berea Board of Trustees challenged the Day Law through the courts. Nevertheless, it was upheld in the Madison Circuit Court in October, 1904, the Kentucky Court of Appeals in June, 1906, and the United States Supreme Court in November, 1908.[8]

In addition to combating discriminatory measures, Kentucky blacks faced other severe challenges, with lynching perhaps the most consistent and troubling. The exact number of blacks lynched in Kentucky from the end of the Civil War to 1940 will never be known because some of them were never reported. During these years at least 353 people died at the hands of lynch mobs. Of this number, 258, or 73 percent, were blacks. It is important to understand that the number of lynchings excludes completely the blacks whose lives were "spared" by the mobs on the promise that the state would quickly execute them.[9]

Indeed, this practice of "Legal Lynchings" was the most difficult violence that blacks encountered because it operated under the sanction of the law. From the Civil War until the 1940s, and indeed later, any number of blacks were tried in hostile environments with judges and juries convinced of their guilt before hearing any evidence. A few "trials" took less than an hour before finding the black defendant guilty and sentencing him to death. In Kentucky, from 1890 to 1940, of the 187 people executed under these circumstances, 106 were blacks. In other words, blacks, comprising no more than 10 percent of the population, accounted for 57 percent of those executed.[10]

Such transgressions against blacks in Kentucky did not go unchallenged. Throughout this period that saw the institutionalization of Jim Crow and increased violence, blacks in the Bluegrass State sought the means to resist. The NAACP became the driving force of the civil rights movement in Kentucky. From its start in Kentucky in 1914, the organization had protested lynchings and mob violence, Jim Crow public transportation, residential segregation, and discrimination in public education. During the late 1920s, the NAACP became involved in a case in the small community of Allensville, in western Kentucky, when a precinct official refused to allow a black man, Samuel Smith, to cast his ballot in the primary election. With the aid of the NAACP's national office, Smith secured the services of a white attorney from Russellville. A court date was scheduled, but in return for Smith dropping the suit, the defendant agreed to pay Smith's attorney's fees and court costs, and not to restrict him or other blacks from voting. This was an important victory for the NAACP.[11]

Making inroads against the state's dual school system presented a great challenge to the NAACP. On one occasion Charles H. Houston, chief legal counsel for the NAACP, received a report from Harry M. Jones, an attorney in Wheeling, West Virginia, about black education in Kentucky. In December, 1937, Jones concluded: "I am satisfied from my cursory review of this subject that in Kentucky we have a glaring example of perhaps the rottenest bi-racial school arrangement in this country; . . . that Kentucky is not square with its Negro children, and that they cannot have under such a set up equal and necessary facilities."[12] In other words, the officials of the NAACP knew that they would encounter staunch resistance from white Kentuckians when attempting to desegregate the public schools.

Several attempts to desegregate higher education occurred in Kentucky in the mid-1930s. That they failed can be blamed on the opposition of the governors and other state officials who became adept at delaying desegregation. Albert Benjamin "Happy" Chandler served as governor during the first of these attempts in 1936. Historians have not written the last word on Chandler and race relations. He has been applauded for being the commissioner of major league baseball to break the color barrier. Yet a recent scholar suggests that Chandler actually had very little to do with the Brooklyn Dodgers signing Jackie Robinson.[13] Regardless of Chandler's stance in 1947, it is clear that during the 1930s, he was no more willing than other Kentucky politicians to dismantle the state's Jim Crow practices. Kentucky's black press repeatedly criticized Chandler for refusing to speak out against mob rule and lynchings and the deplorable state of black schools during his campaign for governor in 1935. After the election, Chandler and his associates stated publicly that the black vote had been cast for his opponent, implying that he owed no political debt to blacks.[14]

Shortly after assuming office, Chandler was approached by Charles W. Anderson, the chief legal counsel of the NAACP in Kentucky, about the admission of black graduate students to the University of Kentucky. His reply is well known: "Such will not happen in your time nor mine." One interpretation of Chandler's statement might be that school desegregation, though a desirable goal, was unlikely to occur given the desire of white Kentuckians for segregated institutions. A more likely interpretation was that the governor did not favor such a radical step. Indeed, when prodded by Anderson, Chandler pointedly refused to endorse desegregation of the state university.[15]

Chandler's commitment to segregation surfaced again three years later, when Alfred M. Carroll, a black twenty-year-old native of Louisville, applied for admission to the University of Kentucky Law School. A graduate of Wilberforce College in Ohio, Carroll was attending Howard University's law school but desired to return home to complete his legal training. Carroll's application led to action from Chandler. From his Emergency Fund, Chandler allocated sixteen hundred dollars to the fund established by the state to send black students to graduate and professional schools in other states. Previously, Chandler had refused to increase the money in this fund, even though black leaders had argued that the money in the fund was insufficient to meet the demand. Along with this action, the governor made one of his harsher statements and warned blacks against demanding admission to the University of Kentucky.[16]

In a letter to Carroll, Alvin E. Evans, dean of the law school, explained that Carroll's application had been denied for two reasons: first, because of Kentucky's laws against school integration, and second, because he had not graduated from an accredited college.[17] After a thorough review of the Carroll case, Thurgood Marshall of the NAACP, strongly advised Charles Anderson to drop the case. Marshall wrote: "The Dean of the Law School took the position that since Carroll was a graduate of Wilberforce and since Wilberforce was not an accredited school, then there might be difficulties in admitting him. . . . We are of the opinion that we should not follow this case through of a technicality that Wilberforce is not an accredited school." Marshall, concerned about the momentum of the NAACP in its college desegregation cases, knew well that a defeat in court would set back the entire cause. Surely another candidate could be found to desegregate the University of Kentucky, he concluded.[18]

Such a candidate appeared in October, 1941, when seventeen-year-old Charles Eubanks, an honor student from Louisville Central High School, filed suit in Fayette Circuit Court, seeking admission to the University of Kentucky School of Engineering. Eubanks explained that he applied to the state university because none of the black colleges offered civil engineering. The assistant state attorney general's comments about the Eubanks's suit foreshadowed the position that the university and state officials would adopt: "The Attorney General's office believes it is a part of an organized effort to stir up class feelings. The colored people and the white people have been getting along fine in

Kentucky and we don't like the idea of stirring things up." Charles W. Anderson and his law partner, Prentice Thomas, were hired as counsel for Eubanks. Throughout the case they relied on the assistance of the NAACP's Thurgood Marshall.[19]

At the urging of Gov. Keen Johnson and University of Kentucky president Herman L. Donovan, an engineering school was promptly created at Kentucky State College. State officials openly acknowledged that the program was an attempt to prevent the desegregation of the University of Kentucky by providing separate but equal opportunities. The admission requirements at both the white and black schools were the same. Students enrolling in engineering courses at Kentucky State were to be charged the same fees as those at the white school.[20] After reviewing the engineering program at Kentucky State, several spokesmen for the University of Kentucky proclaimed that Eubanks's suit was moot, that the state had provided separate but equal facilities for blacks. The NAACP, however, had a vastly different view of the engineering program: "It was found on inspection that the Engineering School at Kentucky State has only one teacher, not an engineer, but a bachelor of science in industrial education. The school is practically without equipment. The curriculum is not an engineering course but an industrial course which includes such subjects as welding." Eubanks refused to attend the school.[21]

To forestall the Eubanks case, the state relied on delaying tactics for over three years. This strategy proved successful when the suit was dismissed due to a lack of prosecution. Kentucky law permitted the dismissal of any case if no action occurred over a two-year period and state officials managed to stall the proceedings long enough. Thurgood Marshall called the outcome of the Eubanks case an "awful licking."[22]

Defeat in the Eubanks case made the NAACP more determined than ever to make its next attempt to desegregate the state university a solid case, with an applicant of unquestionable credentials. It took three years, but on March 15, 1948, Louisville school teacher Lyman T. Johnson applied for admission to the graduate program in history at the University of Kentucky. A native of Tennessee, Johnson held an A.B. degree from Virginia Union University, an M.A. degree from the University of Michigan, and had taken a number of courses toward a Ph.D. at the University of Wisconsin. Upon arriving in Louisville in the early 1930s, he became involved with the NAACP, even serving as president, a step normally not taken by public school employees. In Johnson, the NAACP had found a person with the right educational background and who would not quit for any reason.[23]

These two attributes of Johnson became very important because the University of Kentucky was determined to resist. Upon rejecting his application, university officials released a statement to the press that read: "Our policy has been pretty well defined. We are prohibited by State law and the State Constitution from accepting the registration of a Negro." University officials, as they had in the Eubanks challenge, then went on the offensive, calling for "equal" opportunities for blacks at Kentucky State. The governor did his part, giving Kentucky State twenty-five thousand dollars from his emergency fund to help develop new undergraduate and graduate courses.[24]

By July, 1948, only a few months after Johnson had applied for admission to the state university, new courses were offered at Kentucky State. Black teachers also put pressure on the university. Desiring to take courses in the summer, they applied to various departments at the University of Kentucky. The departments, in turn, selected students for admission but channeled them to summer school at Kentucky State. Professors at the University of Kentucky sent bibliographies to Kentucky State and aided the black school in selecting books for the library. With graduate courses at Kentucky State now providing an alternative to leaving the state for graduate training, thirty blacks, including Lyman Johnson, enrolled in the summer of 1948. White professors from the University of Kentucky drove to Frankfort to teach the courses.

Nevertheless, Johnson and the NAACP continued pressing for his right to attend the state university. The suit stated that Johnson's application had been rejected solely because of his race. At the pretrial conference the NAACP raised three issues: whether provisions had been made for the education of Negroes in the graduate school at Kentucky State; whether the provisions allegedly made by the defendants for the graduate education of Negroes in Frankfort satisfied the Fourteenth Amendment; and whether any facilities established on the basis of segregation solely because of race or color could satisfy the requirements of the Fourteenth Amendment. The University of Kentucky argued that because of the graduate programs at Kentucky State, the willingness of the state to purchase books for Kentucky State's library, and the arrangement of the professors traveling to Frankfort, equality existed for blacks in education.[25]

As the trial approached, the NAACP took steps to strengthen its case. Experts from a wide range of disciplines were prepared to testify that the books and facilities at Kentucky State were inadequate and could not compare with those at the state university. Since Lyman Johnson sought a graduate degree in history, the NAACP decided to have the nation's foremost black historian, John Hope Franklin of Howard University, testify regarding the value of the training Johnson might receive at Kentucky State:

> We would like from you testimony showing the need for an extensive library in order to pursue the subjects which Johnson desires to take; the value in having other students in a class with him, they would be able to interchange ideas, the necessity for having professors available for consultation and assistance after hours; the necessity for having an extensive library within easy access over and above whatever bibliography might be furnished by UK.

Franklin traveled to Lexington for the trial, although he was not called to testify. Nevertheless, Franklin's presence showed the thoroughness of NAACP's preparation for the case.[26]

On March 30, 1949, Judge H. Church Ford of the United States District Court reached a quick decision, a judgment in favor of Lyman Johnson and the NAACP. He said, "How can anyone listen to this evidence without seeing that it is a makeshift plan?" The University of Kentucky was under an obligation to admit qualified black students, Judge Ford forcefully explained, since the state had failed to provide graduate and professional schools for blacks that in any respect equaled the university for whites. That summer, Johnson and thirty other blacks desegregated the University of Kentucky.[27]

After the successful completion of the Johnson suit, the NAACP called for the admission of blacks to all colleges in Kentucky, but the decades-old Day Law remained a barrier for the time being. One year later, however, in 1950, the state legislature handed a death blow to the Day Law and allowed colleges on both the undergraduate and graduate levels to desegregate at their own choosing. Immediately thereafter, several Catholic colleges in Louisville announced the admission of black students and the closing of Louisville Municipal College for Negroes.[28]

With the success of college desegregation, Kentucky black leaders, like the NAACP and others nationally, next moved to public school desegregation in the early 1950s. Because of the logistics involved, the attitude of most whites to "go slow" and, perhaps most importantly, the Supreme Court decision to postpone for a year its final ruling on how school desegregation was to proceed, the dual school system remained intact for the school year 1954–55. Nevertheless, the *Brown* decision influenced Kentucky's education. By mid-1955, after the Court's ruling in "Brown II," (where the justices were purposefully vague, saying that desegregation was to occur with "all deliberate speed"), the first tentative steps toward school desegregation were taken in the state. The Kentucky Department of Education issued a directive to all public school districts to move rapidly to end school segregation. All districts, at the very least, were to begin studying ways of implementing the court decision and working with community leaders.[29]

While applauding the work of the Kentucky Department of Education and positive comments made by white Kentuckians, the NAACP was determined to push for immediate integration or, at the very least, the completion of a desegregation plan with deadlines for school integration. As Roy Wilkins, executive secretary of the NAACP, noted, "Kentucky is one of the key states. We expect it to move off in a good fashion, helping to bring pressure on public opinion against those loudly publicized areas which are resisting the Court's opinion." Realizing that a successful lawsuit would go a long way toward school desegregation in Kentucky, the NAACP carefully investigated all of the school districts and filed suit in federal court on September 1, 1955, against the Columbia school district. Attorney James A. Crumlin, state president of the NAACP, argued that the twenty-five blacks of high school age living in Columbia must be admitted to the white high school. Board members countered by explaining that the high school was already overcrowded with its 541 white students, and desegregation would create additional problems that had to be resolved before blacks could be admitted to Columbia High. On December 1, Federal District Judge Mac Swinford ruled that the high school in Columbia must open its doors to black students on February 1, and that the elementary school would be desegregated when school started in September, 1956. Going further, the judge forcefully argued that the education of all young people was so important in American society that the learning process could not be delayed, and that overcrowded conditions simply was not a valid excuse.[30]

Two highly publicized events occurred during the school year of 1956–57: the sending of the National Guard to protect black students at Sturgis and the peaceful entrance of blacks into the white public schools in Louisville. On Friday, August 31, eight black students enrolled in Sturgis High School. The following Tuesday, the first day of class, the black students were blocked from entering the school by a white mob estimated at about three hundred. The students, unsure of what steps to take, returned home. Members of the school board and city officials refused to stop the mob, though several white leaders said that the black students were actually not threatened with violence. The next day, however, Gov. Albert B. Chandler (who had been re-elected for a second term in 1955, after serving in the United States Senate and as commissioner of major league baseball) ordered the state police and the Kentucky National Guard to Sturgis. Many Kentuckians praised Chandler's actions, saying that he had prevented bloodshed, while others proclaimed just as loudly that it was a grandstand move on his part. In the presence of more than one thousand angry whites, including many outside segregationists who came to Sturgis to lend their support, the black students entered the school on September 6 under protection of two hundred heavily armed guardsmen. For the next week, blacks attended Sturgis High under these conditions, while more than 50 percent of the white students boycotted the school. Eventually, the state attorney general ruled that, since the school board had failed to develop a definite integration plan, the black students were prohibited from further attendance at the school. Acting on this advice, the school board voted to bar the blacks until a satisfactory plan had been formulated. The black students remained determined to attend the school, but on September 19, they were refused admission by the principal, to the delight of the white mob. Rather than return to Dunbar, the black high school, the eight students chose to remain out of school for the entire academic year. The following school year, the Sturgis Board of Education closed the black high school and transferred all black students to Sturgis High. Unlike in 1956, no racial incidents occurred in 1957 when blacks were admitted to the school.[31]

Undeterred by the threat of a violent outbreak in Sturgis, the Louisville Board of Education launched its desegregation plan that same September. For more than a year, the Louisville NAACP had denounced the school board for delaying the start of school integration. Superintendent Omer Carmichael had ignored criticism by blacks, saying that it was important for the desegregation plan to be well in place before proceeding. It is clear from all of his actions that Carmichael wanted whites' approval of school integration. Though his desegregation plan contained several parts, including the redistricting of all of the students to the school closest to their homes, his scheme actually relied on "permissiveness," with the school board opposing compulsory segregation and integration. Under Carmichael's plan, "freedom of choice" was all-important. Blacks could, if they desired, attend mixed (desegregated) schools while whites could attend all-white schools. Because of housing patterns in Louisville, there were many all-white residential areas, and the whites living in close proximity to blacks could easily avoid integration by sending their children to schools in the exclusive white districts. Though the Louisville School System was widely heralded in 1957 for peacefully desegregating its schools, very little integration occurred, with only a few blacks enrolling in white schools and no whites going to black schools.[32]

Given these halting attempts to establish plans for integrating schools and to implement these plans, schools in Kentucky did desegregate over the next decade—at least on paper. By the school year of 1964–65, 95.2 percent of the school districts had desegregated. Eleven school districts with small black populations continued to operate segregated schools, and they took great pains to reassure state education officials that school integration was "forthcoming." In reality, several mountain school districts simply evaded the law, sending their black students to other school districts instead of admitting them to white schools. The desegregation plans from Glasgow, Mount Sterling, and Montgomery County school districts were extremely vague (probably on purpose), saying that blacks enjoyed the privilege of attending the mixed or all-black schools, though it seems as if the only option given blacks was to remain in all-black schools. And despite the repeated threats of the NAACP, Shelby County, which had a large black population, resisted desegregation until the mid-1960s. Only one community in the entire state—Graves County—had failed to adopt a desegregation plan, though officials from the area, fully aware of the court's mandate of "all deliberate speed," consistently expressed their willingness to begin investigating steps that would lead to interracial schools. The failure of school desegregation in Graves County, however, was no surprise because blacks had experienced much violence and racial discrimination in this western Kentucky community since the Civil War.[33]

Significantly, upon close examination, many school boards, though claiming that integration had taken place, had blacks attending only a few of its schools. Not only was this the case in Louisville, but in Lexington as well. As Kentucky's most noted historian, Thomas D. Clark, explained, "Lexington made fewer plans and embarked on desegregation of its schools on a less extensive scale than Louisville. In 1966 the United States Office of Education was critical of what had been accomplished in the Lexington area in light of the new mandates of the Civil Rights Law of 1964." In an attempt to conform to the law, school officials changed a former all-black school into a junior high school for all students and sent black high school students to a previously all-white school. This move greatly upset many white parents who opposed sending their children to the junior high since it was located in a black neighborhood. Eventually the Lexington Board of Education closed all of the schools in black communities, meaning that whites attended schools in close proximity to their homes while blacks were compelled to travel great distances to schools.[34]

Integrating the public schools was not the only goal of the civil rights movement that gained momentum after the *Brown* decision. These same years witnessed efforts by blacks and a handful of liberal whites to achieve equal access to public accommodations. Desegregating the downtown areas in Kentucky's cities proved to be a difficult struggle. In Louisville, a city that prided itself on being "liberal," more than three and one-half years of negotiating and demonstrating—including a boycott of white merchants during the Easter season of 1961 and the exertion of political power by blacks—were necessary to desegregate all of the businesses. Lexington experienced similar demonstrations before conditions changed there in 1963. Achieving equal accommodations in smaller cities was much more problematic, and black leaders realized that only intervention by the state legislature could insure success. Accordingly, they urged Gov. Burt Combs, who had consistently expressed sympathy for the goals of the civil rights movement, to throw the weight of his office behind a measure to end all vestiges of Jim Crow in Kentucky. Governor Combs called upon the General Assembly to act, but was informed by leaders of the house and senate that an anti-discrimination law stood no chance of passing. Determined not to be thwarted by the assembly, on June 26, 1963, the governor issued an executive order that ended racial discrimination in all establishments and professions licensed by the state. This broad ordinance covered virtually every area of secular activity in Kentucky, "outside of the private homes of citizens."[35]

The struggle to achieve access to public accommodations foreshadowed the strong opposition blacks encountered when protesting discrimination in employment and housing. Indeed, in a real sense, the victory in the public accommodations phase was a moderate one: blacks were asking for the right to spend their money in white establishments. Furthermore, the considerable pressure exerted by blacks forced the governor to act to break down the intransigence of whites on the issue. Not surprisingly, therefore, many whites viewed the call by blacks for equal employment opportunities as a real threat to themselves and their livelihood. Many whites who had been sympathetic to the movement to end public accommodation discrimination assumed that employment opportunities were based on education and merit, not race, and that once blacks had acquired the right skills they would face no problems in this area. Housing also met strong resistance. Some whites were opposed to blacks living in their neighborhoods solely on racial grounds. Others were unconvinced that discrimination excluded blacks from white communities. They believed, in spite of any evidence of discrimination uncovered by blacks, that it was in the economic best interest of realtors to sell homes to anyone willing to pay the price to move into certain neighborhoods. Thus, what kept blacks out of white neighborhoods was the inability to meet housing costs.

Just how difficult it was for blacks to move into well-to-do neighborhoods emerged from a 1958 account by socialist Ann Braden. In this very dramatic account, Andrew Wade, a successful black businessman, found it impossible to purchase a decent house in Louisville in the early 1950s. There were two problems: Louisville was a town of "unspoken restrictive covenant," effectively keeping blacks out of white neighborhoods. Secondly, no new housing for blacks had been constructed since before World War II. Wade, an associate of Carl and Ann Braden in an interracial organization, had the couple purchase a home for him in the all-white suburb of Shively in 1954. Immediately after it became known that Wade and his family, not the Bradens, lived in the house there were demands that they vacate the area. The builder, James Rone, and the bank holding the mortgage tried to find violations in the contract that the Bradens had committed in transferring the house to Wade in hopes of voiding the sale. The Bradens, of course, were accused of being Communist agents. Wade, an electrician in business with his father, saw his company suffer as economic pressure was applied to force him to move from Shively. On Saturday night, May 15, ten shots were fired into his home. The house was damaged, but the Wades refused to move. Meanwhile, the Bradens were also the targets of white abuse, even from the usually reasoned and moderate voice of the *Courier-Journal*, which blamed them for the May 15 violence. The drama reached a peak on the night of June 27, when Wade's house was substantially damaged by a bomb. All of the white residents on the street had been warned of the impending bombing and had left their homes. Failing to apprehend the bombers, the police blamed the Bradens for the violence, saying that it had been a ploy on their part to win support for the Communist cause. Carl Braden was arrested, convicted, and sent to prison on a state sedition law. Sentenced to fifteen years in prison and fined five thousand dollars, he was eventually freed in April, 1956, when the United States Supreme Court overturned Kentucky's sedition laws. Wade and his family never returned to the house; in August, 1957, he put up a For Sale sign and eventually sold the property.[36]

Wade's story is unique. The vast majority of blacks did not challenge segregated neighborhoods in such a confrontational mode. What his story makes clear is that in the mid-1950s most white Kentuckians were willing to break the law in order to sidestep integration. In this, they were not so different from whites throughout the nation. It took another ten years for the federal government and the state of Kentucky to enact laws to end racial discrimination in housing, and even then such legislation faced controversy and strong opposition. A far-reaching piece of legislation, Title VIII of the 1968 Civil Rights Act, was designed to end virtually every type of discrimination in housing. The major problem with Title VIII, like so much of the legislation passed during the civil rights movement, became enforcement of the law. Shortly after the law went into effect, an official for the Housing Information Service in Louisville noted, "Ordinance or no ordinance, finding homes for Negroes is hard." As numerous surveys of housing discrimination attest, this remained the case throughout the next decade, and up to the present.[37]

Throughout the civil rights movement, black leaders called for increased employment opportunities for their race, and without question, the mid-1960s witnessed breakthroughs regarding employment. Practically every city publicized the "first black" to be employed in certain jobs. This was most apparent in government jobs on the local and state levels. However, employment breakthroughs for blacks can be easily overstated. For, in reality, many of the changes were token or they affected only the very small percentage of blacks holding advanced degrees. In practically every year of the 1970s, the Kentucky Commission of Human Rights published data on black employment in the public and private sector. These well-researched reports painted a dismal picture, explaining in great detail that in most areas of private employment blacks were completely excluded from managerial positions. Furthermore, the employment gains that they made went largely to men as black women remained underemployed in the work force. Also, though institutions of higher education had declared a strong desire to find and secure the services of qualified blacks as professors and administrators, very few blacks had been hired in Kentucky's colleges and universities. For example, at the University of Kentucky, the University of Louisville, and other predominantly white state universities and colleges, only a small fraction of the faculty—numbering no more than 1 or 2 percent—were black throughout the 1970s. Another revealing look at black employment in many Kentucky cities can be gleaned from local histories, like the one on Henderson, which have been published in the last decade. In Henderson, and elsewhere, very few blacks have been hired as policemen, firemen, or for administrative and secretarial jobs in Henderson city government. By 1980, such communities had no black workers while others had only one in each department of city government. A journey through any

Kentucky city indicates that even fewer changes have occurred in the private sector, especially above entry-level positions. This is especially true in Louisville, Lexington, and Frankfort as blacks still remain mired in service and lower-level jobs. In the final analysis, black progress in employment has occurred but has fallen far short of the expectations of the civil rights movement. Furthermore, many of the gains proved to be short-lived as blacks were the first to experience layoffs and unemployment when the economy worsened in the state and nation during the late 1970s and early 1980s.[38]

In 1966, Frank Stanley, the editor of a black weekly newspaper in Louisville, wrote an article, "The Negro in Kentucky: Is His Apparent Progress More Apparent Than Real," assessing the status of blacks. According to Stanley, on the surface blacks were making tremendous progress in the state, but the facts showed this to be far from the case. Blacks remained relegated to low-paying jobs and living in segregated neighborhoods and slums. He pointed out that: "Negroes generally—the masses—have not benefitted greatly from local, state and federal civil-rights laws. The barometer is the widening of the economic gap between Negroes and whites both on a per capita and a per family average." In a very strongly worded passage, Stanley further explained:

> Frankly, the average Caucasian Kentuckian is mostly unaware of the important goals yet to be achieved, or more specifically, of the amount of non-progress that has been made. Certainly most are totally incapable of realizing the tortures of hellish racial prejudice and what it does to the souls and minds of people who are forced to suffer it. . . . The plain truth is, regardless of how many civil rights laws we pass, Negroes cannot win complete equality or total integration without broad crash programs for full employment, abolition of slums, the reconstruction of our education system and new definitions of work and leisure.[39]

As we look back on the civil rights movement in Kentucky, there is much in Stanley's assessment that rings as true in the 1990s as it did in 1966. The civil rights movement there, as elsewhere, has led to two black Americas. One group of blacks received the very best education and eventually enjoyed what seemed to be unlimited employment opportunities. On the other hand, the vast majority of blacks seems to have been missed entirely by the civil rights movement and exist in a world that has changed little since 1950. In other words, just like blacks throughout the nation, Kentucky blacks during the civil rights movement experienced both meaningful change and continuity.

Yet, many scholars studying the civil rights movement have ultimately reached a more positive conclusion about the success of the movement. In the early years of this century, whites killed blacks at will, denied them anything approaching legal redress, and took their property with impunity. To a very, very significant degree all of these horrible acts have ended. To be sure, racism is more subtle, more covert. But, the fact that racism is now subtle actually means real progress has occurred. In short, the civil rights movement in Kentucky and elsewhere brought hope to blacks, that since they had successfully challenged Jim Crow laws, mob violence, and "legal lynchings," maybe other vestiges of racism could be conquered.

NOTES

*This essay is a condensed version of chapters 4 and 5 of Professor Wright's forthcoming book, *A History of Blacks in Kentucky: In Pursuit of Equality, 1890–1980* (Frankfort: Kentucky Historical Society, 1992).

1. Letter from Henderson Library to American Association, Mar. 22, 1917, letter from Henderson Library to James Bertram, secretary to the Carnegie Corporation, n.d., both in Local History Collection, Henderson Public Library, Henderson, Ky.; Maralea Arnett, *The Annals and Scandals of Henderson County, Kentucky, 1775–1975* (Corydon, Ky.: Fremar Publishing Company, 1976), p. 100.

2. "Along the Color Line," *The Crisis* 3 (Dec., 1911): 54; "The Horizon," *The Crisis* 15 (Apr., 1918): 293; *Louisville Leader*, July 13, 1930. Founded in 1910 and edited by Dr. W. E. B. DuBois until 1934, *The Crisis* is the official journal of the National Association for the Advancement of Colored People (NAACP). In each issue of *The Crisis*, the editors did a national summary of black progress in education, health care, public facilities, etc. The summaries were listed in "Along the Color Line" and in "The Horizon."

3. Letter from P. H. Kennedy and others to the Committee of Ladies Having Charge of Barret Park, Sept. 7, 1903, Henderson Public Library Collection, Henderson, Ky.; Charles M. Meacham, *A History of Christian County* (Nashville: Marshall and Bruce Company, 1930), pp. 360–61. *The Crisis* is an excellent source for information on park segregation in Kentucky cities. See, "Along the Color Line," *The Crisis* 8 (Oct., 1914): 273; "Along the Color Line," *The Crisis* 10 (May, 1915): 8; and "The Horizon," *The Crisis* 12 (Sept., 1916): 247. See also, George C. Wright, *Life behind a Veil: Blacks in Louisville, Kentucky, 1865–1930* (Baton Rouge: Louisiana State University Press, 1985), pp. 274–80.

4. Recorded Deeds of Henderson, Book 50, p. 12, Henderson City Hall, Henderson, Ky. For a discussion of residential segregation ordinances, see W. Ashbie Hawkins, "A Year of Segregation in Baltimore," *The Crisis* 3 (Nov., 1911): 27–30; "Segregation,"

The Crisis 15 (Dec., 1917): 69–73. In the latter *Crisis* article, the *Buchanan* v. *Warley* restrictive covenant case is also reviewed.

5. *Buchanan* v. *Warley*, 245 U.S. 60 (1917); George C. Wright, "The NAACP and Residential Segregation in Louisville, Kentucky, 1914–1917," *Register of the Kentucky Historical Society* 78 (Winter, 1980): 39–54.

6. James D. Anderson, *The Education of Blacks in the South, 1860–1935* (Chapel Hill: University of North Carolina Press, 1988); letter from George Colvin to Robert W. Bingham, Aug. 23, 1923, Robert W. Bingham Papers, Manuscript Division, Library of Congress, Washington, D.C.

7. *Indianapolis Freeman*, May 4, 1899, Dec. 29, 1900. A very important discussion of race relations at Berea can be found in James McPherson, *The Abolitionist Legacy: From Reconstruction to the NAACP* (Princeton, N.J.: Princeton University Press, 1975), chap. 14.

8. See the Day Law File, Berea College Library, Berea, Ky.; *Berea Citizen*, Mar. 17, 24, 1904.

9. George C. Wright, *Racial Violence in Kentucky, 1865–1940: Lynchings, Mob Rule, and "Legal Lynchings"* (Baton Rouge: Louisiana State University Press, 1990), chaps. 1–3.

10. Ibid., chaps. 7–8.

11. Details regarding the entire incident can be found in a letter from Oscar M. Smith, lawyer for Samuel Smith, to W. T. Andrews, of the Legal Department of the NAACP, Aug., 1929, NAACP Administration Files, Box C-285, NAACP Papers, Manuscript Division, Library of Congress, Washington, D.C. The NAACP was also involved in the *Buchanan* v. *Warley* case.

12. Material relating to school desegregation attempts by the NAACP in Kentucky can be found in the NAACP Papers, Group II, Box A232, Manuscript Division, Library of Congress, Washington, D.C.

13. Jules Tygiel, *Baseball's Great Experiment: Jackie Robinson and His Legacy* (New York: Oxford University Press, 1983), pp. 80–86.

14. *Louisville Leader*, Oct. 5, 1935, Nov. 30, 1935, June 25, 1938.

15. Quoted in Kentucky Commission on Human Rights, *Kentucky's Black Heritage* (Frankfort, Ky.: KCHR, 1971), p. 99.

16. *Louisville Courier-Journal*, Jan. 28, 1939, Mar. 12, 1939; *Louisville Leader*, Feb. 4, 1939; letter from Charles W. Anderson to Charles H. Houston, Feb. 8, 1939, NAACP Papers, Manuscript Division, Library of Congress, Washington, D.C.

17. A copy of the letter from Alvin E. Evans to Alfred M. Carroll, Feb. 9, 1939, can be found in the NAACP Papers, Manuscript Division, Library of Congress, Washington, D.C.

18. Letter from Marshall to Anderson, Apr. 5, 1939, NAACP Papers, Manuscript Division, Library of Congress, Washington, D.C.

19. *Louisville Courier-Journal*, Oct. 14, 1941, Oct. 23, 1941; Charles Gano Talbert, *The University of Kentucky: The Maturing Years* (Lexington, Ky.: University of Kentucky Press, 1965) pp. 175–79.

20. A copy of the proposed Engineering Program at Kentucky State can be found in "College Desegregation Suits, 1941," NAACP Papers, Manuscript Division, Library of Congress, Washington, D.C.

21. NAACP Press Release, Apr. 9, 1943; letter from Charles W. Anderson to Walter White, Sept. 1943, NAACP Papers, Manuscript Division, Library of Congress, Washington, D.C.; *Lexington Herald-Leader*, Jan. 24, 1943.

22. *Louisville Defender,* Jan. 13, 1945; letter from Thurgood Marshall to Charles H. Houston, Jan. 16, 1945; Houston to Marshall, Feb. 2, 1945; Marshall to Anderson, Jan. 28, 1945; affidavit of Charles L. Eubanks, Jan. 18, 1945. All of the preceding documents are in the NAACP Papers, Manuscript Division, Library of Congress, Washington, D.C.

23. Interview with Lyman T. Johnson, Mar. 16, 1978, Louisville, Ky.

24. See NAACP Folders on Lyman T. Johnson, Group II, Boxes B-90 to B-150, NAACP Papers, Manuscript Division, Library of Congress, Washington, D.C.

25. Memorandum of Robert L. Carter, assistant special counsel of the NAACP, to Marshall, Mar. 1, 1949, NAACP Papers, Manuscript Division, Library of Congress, Washington, D.C.

26. *Louisville Courier-Journal,* Feb. 17, 1949; Carter to John Hope Franklin, Mar. 23, 1949, NAACP Papers, Manuscript Division, Library of Congress, Washington, D.C.

27. *Lyman Johnson* v. *University of Kentucky;* NAACP Press Release, Mar. 31, 1949; Lyman T. Johnson to Carter, June 29, 1949, all in the NAACP Papers, Manuscript Division, Library of Congress, Washington, D.C.; *New York Times,* June 22, 1949.

28. U.S. House of Representatives, Regular Session 1946, House Bill No. 225, Feb. 1, 1946; *Acts of the General Assembly of the Commonwealth of Kentucky,* chap. 112 (Frankfort, Ky., 1948).

29. Typed memo called "Kentucky" discussed the desegregation process within the state, in NAACP Papers, Manuscript Division, Library of Congress, Washington, D.C.

30. *Fred Willis, et. al.* v. *Herbert Walker, Superintendent of Public Schools, Federal Supplement* 136 (St. Paul, Minn., 1956), 177–85; *Louisville Courier-Journal,* Dec. 2 and 5, 1955.

31. Roscoe Griffin, "A Tentative Description and Analysis of the School Desegregation Crisis in Sturgis, Kentucky, August 31–September 19, 1956." See also a letter from Roscoe Griffin to Gov. Albert B. Chandler, Feb. 8, 1957. Both documents can be found in the Albert B. Chandler Papers, Department of Special Collections, University of Kentucky, Lexington.

32. Omer Carmichael, *The Louisville Story* (New York: Simon & Schuster, 1958); Darlene Walker, "Preparation for the Desegregation of the Louisville School System," Master's thesis, University of Louisville, 1974.

33. *Lexington Herald,* Jan. 29, 1961; *Louisville Courier-Journal,* May 1, 1962, Aug. 23, 1964; Wright, *Racial Violence in Kentucky,* p. 72.

34. Thomas D. Clark, *Kentucky: Land of Contrast* (New York: Harper & Row, 1968), p. 118; John D. Wright, *Lexington: Heart of the Bluegrass* (Lexington, Ky.: Lexington and Fayette County Historical Commission, 1982), pp. 199–200; George H. Yater, *A History of Louisville* (Louisville, Ky.: Heritage Corp., 1979), p. 225.

35. *Louisville Courier-Journal,* June 27, 1963; George C. Wright, "Desegregation of Public Accommodations in Louisville: A Long and Difficult Struggle in a 'Liberal' Border City," in Elizabeth Jacoway and David R. Colburn, eds., *Southern Businessmen and Desegregation* (Baton Rouge: Louisiana State University Press, 1982), pp. 191–210.

36. Ann Braden, *The Wall Between* (New York: Monthly Review Press, 1958).

37. See *United States Codes Annotated* (St. Paul, Minn., 1977), 3601–31.

38. Freida J. Dannheiser and Donald L. Hazelwood, eds., *The History of Henderson County Kentucky* (Evansville, Ind.: Unigraphic, 1980), pp. 61–81; Kentucky Commission on Human Rights (KCHR), *Status of Women in Kentucky State Agencies: An Analysis of Employment and Job Level* (Louisville, Ky.: KCHR, 1972); KCHR, *Black*

Employment in Kentucky State Agencies: An Analysis of Job Levels, Salaries and Hiring Patterns (Louisville, Ky.: KCHR, 1974); KCHR, *State University Faculties Stuck on Tokenism in Kentucky* (Louisville, Ky.: KCHR, 1979); KCHR, *No Blacks Are Near the Top of Louisville Hotel Employment* (Louisville, Ky.: KCHR, 1979).

39. *Louisville Courier-Journal*, Feb. 6, 1966.

W. MARVIN DULANEY

Whatever Happened to the Civil Rights Movement in Dallas, Texas?

DURING the past six years, the city of Dallas has experienced an unusual amount of racial tension over the lack of African-American and Hispanic representation in city government and over the use of deadly force by police officers. Responding to the latter issue, the city's lone African-American county commissioner even called for armed rebellions in the streets, reminiscent of the tactics that African Americans used in other cities during the 1960s.[1] Because of the recent racial tension in Dallas, many believe the civil rights movement bypassed that city. *Dallas Times Herald* columnist Jim Schutze in his book, *The Accommodation*, even contends that African-American leaders subverted the movement by allying with the Dallas Citizens' Council. In this alliance, they sought to manage integration and to prevent racial violence like that which occurred in Little Rock, Birmingham, and New Orleans when those cities began the process of desegregation. Schutze's thesis has some merit, but it does not tell the full story.[2]

Dallas did have a civil rights movement, and the African Americans who participated in it from the 1930s to the 1950s were in the forefront of the ongoing national struggle by Americans of all races to end racial injustice, discrimination, and repression.[3] African Americans in Dallas made the 1930s a watershed not only for the local version of the civil rights movement, but also for the movement throughout the South. After they formed a political organization and an active state chapter of the NAACP, African Americans won two of the landmark civil rights cases in the South. But the movement in Dallas did not fulfill its promise. In the 1960s, African Americans in that city never used tactics of direct action or violence to win the more substantial gains of political and economic power that the movement brought to African Americans in cities such as Atlanta, New Orleans, and Birmingham.

Several historians who have studied race relations in Texas contend that the mass demonstrations and violence that characterized the civil rights movement in other parts of the South did not occur in Texas because the state is not really a part of the Deep South. Allegedly, race relations were moderate in Texas. Therefore, African Americans in various communities throughout the state had only to work with moderate white leadership to negotiate changes in segregation. According to this view, when African Americans began to confront white supremacy in cities throughout the state, they did not have to confront the White Citizens Councils and Ku Klux Klan chapters that were the main sources of resistance to change confronting African Americans in the Deep South.[4]

Despite this view, however, the historical record indicates that African Americans in Texas confronted a racial environment as rigid as that in other parts of the Deep South — a system of racial violence and segregation that was not much different from that which they experienced during slavery. Immediately after the Civil War, white Texans used violence and terror to establish a "new relationship" between African Americans and whites in the state. According to the Freedmen's Bureau commissioners and the Committee on Violence and Lawlessness organized by the Texas Constitutional Convention of 1868, nearly two thousand African Americans were murdered between 1865 and 1868 through random violence, vigilantism, and attempts by former Texas slaveholders to keep them in slavery. Of the homicide victims in that period, 97 percent were African-American males (1 percent of the African-American male population in Texas between the ages of fifteen and forty-nine). This high percentage indicates that white Texans aimed the brunt of their terror against the group of African Americans best able to defend themselves and to challenge the racial status quo disrupted by the war.[5]

The violence against African Americans in Texas continued after Reconstruction and into the twentieth century. Two cases in Dallas serve as examples of this violence. In March, 1910, an elderly black man named Allen Brooks was accused of molesting a three-year-old white child. A mob, which grew to five thousand people, broke into the courthouse, tied a rope around his neck, and threw him out of the courthouse window. He was then dragged through the streets of downtown Dallas, his body mangled as he was dragged along, and then he was hanged from a telephone pole. As the last breath of life left his body, the mob tore off pieces of his clothing, then pieces of the telephone pole, and finally pieces of his mangled body for souvenirs. No one was ever prosecuted for the crime, and both Dallas newspapers gave editorial support to the lynching of Brooks.[6] The second case of violence and terror against African Americans in Dallas, while less gruesome, nevertheless exposes the pattern of racial intimidation that was part of the African-American experience in Dallas. In April, 1921, fifteen members of the Dallas Ku Klux Klan kidnapped young Alexander Johnson. Johnson, a bell boy in a downtown hotel, allegedly had bragged about having sexual relations with some of the white women guests. For his offense, the Klan whipped him and branded his forehead with the letters *KKK*. Two newspaper reporters were also kidnapped with Johnson and forced to watch the whipping and branding in order to report the incident to the community as a warning to any other African-American men who had ideas about having relationships with white women. Just as in the Brooks case, no one was ever prosecuted; indeed, it seems likely that some of his kidnappers were members of the Dallas police department because, according to an extant list of Klan members on the police force in 1921, every member of the force, from the police commissioner down, was a member of the Ku Klux Klan.[7] Admittedly, Brooks's and Johnson's cases were two of the more sensational ones; nevertheless, they show how precarious life was for African Americans who challenged the prevailing racial norms.

There was also a general pattern of apartheid that affected all aspects of African-American life in Dallas. Just as in other parts of the South, the apartheid system in Dallas developed almost immediately after the Civil War and affected African Americans' access to housing, law enforcement, voting, public facilities, health care, and employment. White Democrats helped to establish apartheid in Texas by eliminating African-American voters from state politics. A poll tax, passed in 1902, and the Democrats' white primary law, passed in 1903, achieved this objective. These laws reduced the number of African Americans voting in Texas from more than one hundred thousand in the 1890s to fewer than five thousand by 1906. With no real political power to protect their rights, African Americans were at the mercy of white Texans. As a result, over the first three decades of this century, the city of Dallas systematically and deliberately circumscribed the social and political lives of the African-American population. In 1907, the city of Dallas revised its charter to establish segregation of the races in all aspects of city life: in public schools, housing, amusements, and churches. The city further restricted where African Americans could live by adopting a charter amendment in 1916 that provided for residential segregation. Another city charter amendment in 1930 also restricted the access of African Americans to the political process because it required all candidates for city government offices to run at large and on a nonpartisan basis, which effectively prevented blacks from winning office. Under this second charter amendment, the city council also furthered apartheid by passing an ordinance to segregate the races on public transportation.[8]

Despite the establishment of an apartheid system in Dallas, the experience of African Americans was not one of complete victimization. Many African Americans attempted to improve their circumstances by participating in local and state Republican politics. Rev. Alexander Stephens Jackson and attorney Ammon S. Wells were active in Republican politics in Dallas County, and they fought the movement by some white Republicans to eliminate African Americans from the party in order to win white votes. In the late nineteenth and early twentieth centuries, African Americans also petitioned the Dallas City Council repeatedly for better law enforcement and for a share of publicly funded jobs in their neighborhoods, but their petitions were usually ignored. In addition, in 1918, African Americans in Dallas formed a chapter of the NAACP, which was led by George F. Porter, a Dallas schoolteacher, and Ammon S. Wells. Porter, who was especially brave, was one of the first teachers in Dallas to protest against the unequal pay that African-American teachers earned for doing the same job as white teachers. In the early 1920s, however, the Klan-dominated police department intimidated the Dallas NAACP virtually out of existence by mandating that a Dallas police officer be allowed to attend all NAACP meetings to observe activities.[9]

Apartheid in Dallas also did not prevent African Americans from maintaining a viable and progressive community. They established and maintained businesses, churches, and even a long-running newspaper. By the mid-1920s, a small middle class emerged in the city—teachers, doctors, lawyers, and other professionals serving the African-American population. In 1926, several of them founded the Dallas Negro Chamber of Commerce in an effort to promote business development and to improve the living standards of the city's African-American population.[10]

By the beginning of the 1930s, improving the living standards of blacks became crucial. In addition to suffering the negative economic effects of the depression, Dallas's African-American community was plagued by poor housing, unpaved streets, lackadaisical law enforcement, and a general neglect of living standards by the city government. A county judge even urged white voters to oppose a city bond issue because it would provide a free library for African Americans. This attitude of neglect extended to education as well. The lone African-American high school, Booker T. Washington, was seriously overcrowded, with 1,664 students attending a facility designed for a maximum of 600. Moreover, African Americans claimed they did not receive their fair share of federal government relief efforts promised under the New Deal.[11]

All of these problems had existed for decades, but the Great Depression exacerbated them. Thus, the 1930s became a watershed in Dallas because African Americans began to attack the problems of crime, poor and inadequate housing, and insufficient school facilities. They also sought to improve the city services that they received and to participate in the political process. Three significant and related events occurred in the 1930s to facilitate the new approach that African Americans took toward their political empowerment and their struggle for civil rights: in 1932, the Dallas Negro Chamber of Commerce hired A. Maceo Smith as Executive Secretary; in 1936, a cross section of African-American social and civic groups organized the Progressive Voters League (PVL); and in the same year, new members of the Dallas chapter of the NAACP, such as Smith and Juanita Craft, revived that organization and made it part of a statewide civil rights campaign.

The Dallas Negro Chamber of Commerce hired Smith as executive secretary to rejuvenate the organization and begin a permanent program of economic and political activities in the African-American community. Smith was from Texarkana and was a 1924 graduate of Fisk University. He had also earned a master's degree from New York University in 1928. He arrived in Dallas in 1932 and began to reorganize the chamber. One of his major accomplishments was to involve the chamber in the Texas Centennial of 1936 and to secure funds to build the Hall of Negro Life at the Centennial State Fair. Smith was also instrumental in involving the chamber in politics. He was one of the founders of the PVL and served on the executive committee for over ten years. He left the chamber in 1939 to accept a job as racial relations advisor with the United States Housing Authority. That same year he became president of the Texas State Conference of Branches of the NAACP, leading the organization in undertaking two of the landmark civil rights cases of the 1940s and 1950s.[12]

In 1936, African Americans organized the PVL, the most important political organization founded by African Americans in Dallas until the 1960s. Two events led to the formation of this organization. The first occurred in 1934, when members of Alpha Phi Alpha fraternity (a national fraternity organized in Dallas in 1932 among African-American college graduates) held their annual Education for Citizenship Week program. Participants, who included A. Maceo Smith as a speaker, discussed the meaning of responsible citizenship and concluded that voting and participating in the political process were the key to responsible citizenship as well as the best way to address the needs of Dallas's African-American community. Acting on the enthusiasm generated by the fraternity's program, African Americans formed the Progressive Citizens League to encourage involvement in the political process and the positive use of the ballot to secure the needs of their community. The league held a poll tax payment campaign and initiated a suit in 1934 to open the Democratic primary in Dallas County to African-American voters. A Dallas judge dismissed the suit, however, and denied African Americans the right to participate in the Democrats' primary.[13]

In 1935, a second event encouraged the formation of a political organization. State Representative Sarah T. Hughes resigned to accept a position as county judge, and attorney Ammon S. Wells entered the general election to fill her seat. Wells was a former president of the NAACP and current president of the Progressive Citizens League. His candidacy for the Texas House of Representatives was a bold move for any African American in Texas in the 1930s, sparking controversy in Dallas County and statewide. Whites were annoyed because he had the nerve to run and because he had a good chance of winning—there were *sixty candidates* seeking the office. Wells lost, but he finished sixth and polled 1,001 votes; the winner polled only 1,844 votes. More important, Well's candidacy sent a clear message to such African-American leaders as A. Maceo Smith and Rev. Maynard H. Jackson, pastor of New Hope Baptist Church: if more of Dallas's ten thousand potential African-American voters had registered and voted, Wells might well have won a seat in the state legislature. This fact motivated Smith and Jackson to accelerate their efforts at political organizing—efforts that culminated in the formation of the PVL in 1936.[14]

Led by Rev. Maynard H. Jackson, the PVL had immediate success in the political arena. Jackson, the son of Alexander Stephens Jackson, and the father of Maynard H. Jackson, Jr., who would serve as the mayor of Atlanta, became the first president of the PVL. Before he moved to Atlanta in 1945, he was one of Dallas's leading citizens and became the first African American to run for the Dallas school board. As a minister and member of the powerful Interdenominational Ministerial Alliance (IMA) (an organization that consisted of the city's most prominent African-American clergy), Jackson was the logical choice to lead the PVL and to unite all of the city's African-American civic and social organizations into an organized voting bloc. In April, 1937, this African-American voting bloc led by the PVL cast the deciding votes in the city council election. Its supporters were rewarded when the city council voted to integrate the police force in 1937 and when the city built a new African-American high school in 1939. The PVL continued to attempt to influence local elections by interviewing prospective candidates for office, and by publicly endorsing a slate of candidates for consideration by African-American voters.[15]

The success of African Americans in the political arena was matched by their successes in civil rights cases. Determined to attack apartheid from all sides, A. Maceo Smith, Juanita Craft, and Maynard Jackson reinvigorated the Dallas chapter of the NAACP, which had been virtually defunct since the early-1920s. Holding its first meeting in several years in 1936, the Dallas chapter identified one key area of concern: securing public sector employment for African Americans as police officers, postal workers and sanitation workers. A year later, the organization specified discrimination on buses and street cars as an additional area that its members needed to address. The Dallas NAACP was never strong enough to act on these issues; however, because of the dynamism of A. Maceo Smith, who was named state secretary of the newly organized Texas State Conference of Branches of the NAACP, Dallas became the center of the campaigns to overturn the Democratic white primary, to equalize the salaries of African-American teachers and to integrate the University of Texas.[16]

After Smith became president of the Texas State Conference of Branches of the NAACP in 1939, the organization made plans to pursue another case to overturn the Democrats' white primary. African Americans in Texas had contested the Democrats' white primary three times, but had lost their most recent challenge in 1935, when the United States Supreme Court concurred with the state's argument that the Democrats' primaries were private, organizational businesses and not state action.[17] In 1940, Smith coordinated a statewide campaign to raise eight thousand dollars for another legal challenge of the white primary. The money was never raised; instead Smith, Carter Wesley of the *Houston Informer* chain of newspapers, and attorney W. J. Durham of Dallas contributed most of the money when the NAACP next challenged the white primary. That landmark case centered on Houston dentist, Lonnie E. Smith, who was denied a ballot in the 1940 Harris County Democrats' party primary and took legal action. The NAACP's General Counsel Thurgood Marshall, assisted by W. J. Durham, unsuccessfully argued the case in the United States District Court. The NAACP then appealed to the Supreme Court. Before the United States Supreme Court heard arguments in the *Smith* case in November, 1943, and January, 1944, it ruled on the case of *U.S.* v. *Classic* (1941) and declared that party primaries were an integral part of the political process, and that by holding primaries, political parties carried out state action. After hearing Marshall's and Durham's arguments in the *Smith* case, the Court ruled in favor of the plaintiffs that race could not be used to deny participation in party primaries because white-only primaries violated the Fourteenth and Fifteenth Amendments.[18]

While pursuing and supporting the primary case, African Americans filed suit to equalize the salaries of African-American teachers with those of white teachers. To challenge the inequitable, racially biased salary structure in the city's public schools, African Americans created a new organization, the Dallas Council of Negro Organizations (DCNO). Organized in 1942, the DCNO consisted of all the major African-American organizations in the city: the NAACP, the PVL, the Negro Chamber of Commerce, the IMA, and nineteen other organizations. With the support of the DCNO, attorney W. J. Durham filed the case *Page* v. *Board of Education, City of Dallas* in November, 1942. He won a judgment in the case in February, 1943, which granted pay raises to African-American teachers over a two-year period until their salary level reached that of whites.[19]

With their victories in the white primary and salary equalization cases, African Americans undertook a third case: the desegregation of the University of Texas Law School. A. Maceo Smith later recalled that he sat on his porch with Thurgood Marshall drinking whiskey and discussing whom they might get to file the test case to desegregate the University of Texas Law School. Finding the right candidate was not easy. Marshall, Smith, and other NAACP leaders knew that the success of the case rested largely on the credentials of the student. Finally, Carter Wesley of the *Informer* brought Houston postal worker and Wiley College graduate Heman Marion Sweatt to their attention as the plaintiff for the case. Sweatt applied to the University of Texas Law School in February, 1946, and his application for admission was rejected on the basis of race. Unlike the white primary case, Sweatt's case was truly a grass-roots effort by African Americans in Dallas and throughout the state of Texas. Smith coordinated a fundraising campaign out of the Dallas NAACP office and raised enough money not only to support the case, but also to support Sweatt if and when he gained admission to the University of Texas Law School.[20]

Marshall and Durham filed the *Sweatt* v. *Painter* case requesting that the Texas State Board of Regents admit Sweatt to the University of Texas Law School because no "separate but equal" law school existed in the state for African-American students. Marshall and Durham lost the case in the local courts. While they were appealing the case, the Regents opened "Prairie View Law School for Negroes" in Houston for Sweatt to attend. Marshall and Durham proceeded with Sweatt's case in spite of this subterfuge. They argued that the "new Negro law school" was not equal to the one at the University of Texas and did not have the same quality of facilities, library, faculty, and national accreditation. The United States Supreme Court agreed with Marshall and Durham and, in 1950, ordered the University of Texas to admit Sweatt as a student.[21]

The success of the NAACP in the landmark *Smith* and *Sweatt* cases was matched by a number of gains that African Americans made in Dallas in the 1940s. In 1941, the first African Americans served as jurors after having been barred from jury service for over fifty years. In 1946, they won their first precinct chairs in the Democratic party and participated in the Dallas County Democrats' county convention. During the same year, the Dallas City Council authorized the appointment of fourteen African-American police officers to patrol the city's black neighborhoods. Two African-American police officers went on duty in March, 1947. There were also minor gains such as the appointment of the first African-American postal workers at the Dallas post office, the participation of African Americans in defense industries, and the opening of Wahoo City Park for African Americans.[22]

Despite these successes, crucial problems still faced African Americans in the city. Racial discrimination limited access of the city's growing African-American population to adequate housing. The city's segregated schools also remained a problem, and the Dallas Board of Education even resisted the 1954 Supreme Court school desegregation order. Finally, public facilities remained segregated, and African Americans could not try on clothes in downtown stores. All of these problems remained in spite of the civil rights gains that Dallas's African Americans made in the 1940s. These problems began to fester in the 1950s.

Finding adequate and sufficient housing proved to be the most difficult problem that African Americans faced. Like most southern cities, Dallas was segregated residentially and no homes were built specifically for African Americans. Thus, there was nowhere for African Americans to buy quality housing. Many people were mired in unhealthy slum conditions in the western part of the city along the banks of the Trinity River. In the early 1940s, a number of middle-class African Americans, seeking to escape the poor housing conditions that existed in the areas designated for black residents, bought homes in the South Dallas area along Oakland Boulevard—a transitional area between a white neighborhood and a growing African-American neighborhood. In 1941, whites bombed eighteen homes bought by African Americans in an attempt to drive them from the neighborhood. The Dallas police attempted to protect the homes of African Americans in the area but never apprehended anyone for the bombings. The city of Dallas tried to resolve the matter by buying out African-American homeowners or convincing them to return the homes to the original owners. But more bombings of African-American homes in the same area occurred in 1950 and 1951. Due to a number of protests from African Americans, the police, with the assistance of the Texas Rangers, finally arrested ten suspects; but none of them were ever convicted. The city of Dallas finally acted to build several segregated, public-housing projects for African Americans and an all-black housing subdivision to resolve the crisis that African Americans faced because of the city's policy of residential segregation. Residential segregation thus continued in Dallas unresolved.[23]

African Americans also faced continuation of segregated schools with the inherent inequities in facilities and resources that segregation perpetuated. Aided by the 1954 Supreme Court decision, however, African Americans sought to force the school board to desegregate the city's public school system in 1955. Twenty-eight African-American students attempted to attend white schools in 1955 and were turned away. The Dallas NAACP filed a suit against the board, but the case was continued repeatedly to delay desegregation of the school system.[24]

The Dallas NAACP's case against the school board was one of the cases that precipitated action by white Texans to resist the Supreme Court's school desegregation mandate. All across the South, whites formed White Citizens Councils to resist desegregation and to use "massive resistance" against the NAACP's school desegregation lawsuits. In 1955 whites in Dallas formed a local version of the White Citizens Council and called it the Texas Citizens Council of Dallas. The Texas Citizens Council vowed "to fight to the end to maintain segregation in Texas schools." But the brunt of the resistance and the attack on the NAACP was led by Texas state attorney general John Ben Sheppard.[25] In September, 1956, Sheppard began the state's campaign to outlaw the NAACP, intimidate its leaders, and drive it out of business in Texas. In retaliation for the NAACP's school desegregation suits, he obtained an injunction against the NAACP's activities in Texas, subpoenaed such members of the Texas State Conference of Branches of the NAACP as A. Maceo Smith, and confiscated branch office records throughout the state. His actions had the effect of suspending the operation of the NAACP in Texas for eight months (from September, 1956, to May, 1957). He charged the organization with barratry and failing to file the appropriate documents to do business as a corporation in the state of Texas.[26]

The attorney general's actions had a devastating effect on the Dallas NAACP. Although the NAACP's lawyers won their case against the state's charges, the harassment virtually destroyed the organization, and it took the NAACP more than three years to recover. Once A. Maceo Smith's superiors at the Dallas Federal Housing Authority learned that he was a party in the state's case against the NAACP, he was forced to resign as state executive secretary and to cut ties with the local branch. He also resigned from the NAACP's national board. The national office of the NAACP tried several times to revitalize the organization by sending in a regional officer to hold state meetings and to plan strategy for the school desegregation cases. Eventually, national executive director Roy Wilkins came to Texas to reestablish local chapters and to increase branch membership. But the NAACP in Dallas still languished for two years until Minnie Flanagan became president in 1959 and involved the organization in the Dallas sit-in movement.[27]

Despite its problems, the NAACP continued to pursue the school desegregation case in Dallas. NAACP lawyers had to overcome six years of appeals and delaying tactics by the school board to resist integration. The school board was aided in its resistance by a new state law requiring Texas school districts to hold "integration votes" to determine if local residents favored school integration. According to the state law, if Texas school districts did not hold the referendums, they would lose state funding for education. The Dallas school board held such a referendum on the issue in August, 1960, and voters rejected school "integration" by a four-to-one margin (30,324 to 7,416 votes). Nevertheless, the NAACP continued to press the issue of school desegregation and used its victory in the United States Fifth Circuit Court of Appeals to force the school board to develop a desegregation plan. In 1961, the school board adopted a plan in which schools desegregated one grade a year, starting with the first grade, until all twelve grade levels were desegregated. Eighteen African-American students enrolled in previously all-white elementary schools in August, 1961. This "desegregation" occurred in Dallas without the massive demonstrations and confrontations that had characterized the process in Little Rock, Arkansas, and New Orleans, Louisiana.[28] It also foreshadowed how

African-American and white leadership would handle the process of desegregating public life in Dallas.

The Dallas Citizens Council, a powerful group of white business leaders, handled the school desegregation process in the city as it had other issues that had confronted the city for thirty years. Formed in 1937 by some of the city's most prominent bankers and business leaders, the Citizens Council ruled the city through its surrogate political arm, the Citizens Charter Association (CCA). The Citizens Council sought to provide the city nonpartisan, "good government" and to run the city efficiently for the good of all citizens. The Citizens Council attempted to rule by consensus rather than confrontation, and to solve problems, such as the ongoing shortage of housing for African Americans, by negotiation and private sector involvement rather than government intervention. From its inception, the Citizens Council was successful in negotiating with African-American leadership to achieve minor racial changes (for example, the public housing projects built for African Americans in 1957). African-American leaders responded to the token consideration provided by the Citizens Council by supporting CCA-backed candidates in every city government election from 1939 to 1959, except for two elections. The issue of integration, however, presented the Citizens Council and African-American leadership with a problem that challenged the city's political culture of consensus.[29]

The Citizens Council began to address the problem of desegregation even before the court's decision in the school desegregation case. In March, 1960, NAACP national executive director Roy Wilkins visited Dallas for a regional meeting. His visit occurred just after students in other parts of the South had begun the sit-in movement the previous month. The NAACP had gone on record as supporting the sit-in movement and thus members of the Citizens Council believed that Wilkins was coming to Dallas to organize sit-ins in the city's segregated downtown stores, under the auspices of the NAACP. They requested a meeting with Wilkins and other leaders of the NAACP in an effort to forestall possible confrontations. Wilkins told an interracial group of city leaders that they needed to begin desegregating the city immediately if they wanted to avoid the confrontations occurring in other parts of the South.

Later in March, acting on Wilkins's suggestion, seven African

Americans and seven whites formed the Committee of 14 to negotiate and manage desegregation in Dallas. The whites were members of the Citizens Council and included financier Karl Hoblitzelle (one of the original members of the Citizens Council), bankers James W. Aston, Jr., and W. W. Overton, Dallas Power and Light president C. A. Tatum, insurance executive Carr P. Collins, wholesale liquor distributor Julius Schepps, and industrialist John E. Mitchell. The African Americans were A. Maceo Smith, NAACP attorney W. J. Durham, C. Jack Clark of Black & Clark Funeral Home, tire company executive Ed Reed, businessman Henry Lenoir, Rev. B. E. Joshua, and businessman George Allen. The "Committee of 14" was supported in its work by the Dallas Community Committee (DCC), headed by Rev. E. C. Estell, pastor of St. John's Baptist Church. Organized in August, 1960, the interracial DCC consisted of members of the NAACP, the IMA, and other church and civic groups in the city. The DCC's charge was to carry out the activities for improving race relations and desegregating public life that resulted from the negotiations of the Committee of 14. A. Maceo Smith made regular reports about the Committee of 14's negotiations and decisions to Rev. Estell, who then directed the DCC in implementing and supporting desegregation activities.[30]

Sponsored by the Citizens Council, the Committee of 14 held its first meeting on March 24, 1960, and A. Maceo Smith addressed the group and outlined work that the committee had to do. Smith said that the committee had to open lines of communication among all racial and ethnic groups in the city. The six objectives Smith identified for the Committee to consider were, in his words:

1. Provide unsegregated food service in retail stores.
2. Provide unsegregated accommodations in public facilities.
3. Facilitate wider employment opportunities for Negroes in all City departments.
4. Remove racial designations signs from all public buildings.
5. Establish a policy of non-segregation in seating accommodations at sporting events and in other public places.
6. Open accommodations in hotels and hostelries.[31]

But not all African Americans or whites were willing to let the Committee of 14 set the agenda. While the committee was planning its program of managed desegregation, Dallas had its first sit-in on April 30, when two ministers, Rev. T. D. R. Thompson, African American, and Rev. Aston Jones, white, entered the S. H. Kress and H. L. Green stores in downtown and were served without incident. Caught off guard, the employees of both stores apparently served the two ministers to avoid a confrontation. But after this episode both stores continued their policy of racial segregation and refused to serve African Americans at their lunch counters. As the Committee of 14 continued its measured negotiations, some members of the DCC grew impatient and organized to picket downtown stores that would not serve African Americans, especially the H. L. Green and S. H. Kress stores. In October, 1960, Rev. Rhett James, pastor of New Hope Baptist Church, led the first organized picketing of downtown stores. James involved a cross section of the African-American community in maintaining the picket lines. Each day of the week, a different group was assigned to maintain the picket line: lawyers one day, ministers the next day, business and professional people the next, and beauticians on another day.[32]

The pickets lasted only two months, but the action split the ranks of the DCC. Rev. Estell, chairman of the DCC, indicated his disagreement with picketing lunch counters in a speech in November, 1960; he criticized the picketers and called them ignorant. This fractured his relationship with James, who attacked Estell publicly in an editorial in the *Express*. Responding to Estell's charge that the picketers were ignorant, James pointed out that all segments of the African-American community and even some white civic leaders were participating in the pickets. He charged Estell with duplicity because he had chaired the meeting in which members of the DCC had agreed to use direct-action tactics to desegregate downtown stores. Nevertheless, in December, 1960, the pickets were called off and James resigned from the DCC in protest. The DCC was following Estell's recommendation (and that of African-American members of the "Committee of 14") to end direct-action tactics and continue negotiations at the bargaining table. James's disagreement with the decision revealed the division over tactics among African Americans.[33]

After resigning from the DCC, Rhett James tried to force the DCC to pressure the "Committee of 14" to implement desegregation in the city's public accommodations. He sent the DCC a telegram on January 1, 1961, with the ultimatum that downtown lunch counters be desegregated by January 14, or he would begin immediate direct-action tactics. The DCC failed to respond, and James, several other African

Americans, and more than sixty Southern Methodist University students began a sit-in campaign in downtown stores and at lunch counters on Hillcrest Avenue near the university. The DCC continued its inaction and some of its members became disgruntled and threatened a boycott of downtown stores during Easter. The Easter boycott did not materialize, but in a full-page ad in the May 27, 1961, *Express*, more than three hundred African-American women pledged not to shop in downtown stores until they were accorded the same treatment as other American citizens. They urged all other African-American women to observe the same pledge and to encourage their friends to abide by it.[34]

Negotiations between African-American and white members of the Committee of 14 clearly had stalled after some initial desegregation agreements. But the threatened boycott broke the stalemate. Just ten days after the *Express* ad, A. Maceo Smith reported that the committee had made some progress toward desegregation. He reported that three of the major downtown stores had begun to serve African Americans at their lunch counters. He also reported that the police department had agreed to hire twenty more African Americans as police officers, place them in uniform, assign them to work in all parts of the city, and allow them the use of two patrol cars. Finally, he reported that the committee had secured employment for African Americans in several stores and private companies and had increased the number of African Americans employed by the city.[35]

The Committee of 14 announced its biggest achievement in July, 1961. On July 26, 1961, business establishments in downtown Dallas would remove their discriminating signs, symbols, and practices and extend service to all customers, regardless of race. To dramatize this achievement, the committee arranged for 159 African Americans to walk into 49 downtown lunch counters and restaurants and be served without incident. This action prompted the DCC to call off its boycott.[36]

The Committee of 14 extended its managed desegregation plan to the city's schools. To prepare citizens for school desegregation, the committee produced a film entitled "Dallas at the Crossroads." Narrated by then CBS News anchor Walter Cronkite, and featuring some of Dallas's leading African-American and white citizens, the film stressed the importance of observing the law in order to avoid the racial chaos that had occurred in cities such as Little Rock and New Orleans during school desegregation. The Committee of 14 circulated the film to African-American and white church groups, civic organizations, labor organizations, and showed it on a local television station. The committee also distributed a small booklet to accompany the film to more than one hundred thousand Dallas citizens. School desegregation took place in the fall of 1961 with few complications or incidents.[37]

On the surface, desegregation took place smoothly and with a minimum of racial strife. The managed desegregation plan led by the Committee of 14 appeared to be so successful that state and national leaders lauded the plan, and representatives from other cities came to Dallas to study it. Texas senator John Tower even praised the plan on the floor of the United States Senate. By the time the federal government passed the Civil Rights Act of 1964 mandating the end of discrimination in public accommodations, Dallas leaders were patting themselves on the back for having "solved" the problem in advance of federal action.[38]

In reality, however, the city's desegregation actions were still tokenism. Smith's 1961 report to the DCC also contained evidence of the persistence of segregation and the inability of the committee to force compliance by several downtown stores and public facilities. For example, H. L. Green, S. S. Kresge, and the Union Terminal lunch counters continued to refuse service to African Americans. Bus stations, Parkland Hospital, and the Texas State Fair continued their policies of racial discrimination. The tokenism in the managed integration plan was most evident in the slow pace of school desegregation. In violation of the law and the 1961 Court of Appeals decision, the school board began construction of another all-black high school in 1962. Moreover, even in the mid-1960s, African-American schoolteachers still faced intimidation or dismissal for participating in NAACP activities.[39] The Committee of 14 worked to resolve these problems, and except for the continuation of school and housing segregation, eventually resolved most of them. But the continued existence of segregation and discrimination and the committee's policy of discouraging dissent and direct-action tactics eventually led some African Americans to challenge the city's established political culture of negotiating change. They would also legitimately charge that desegregation was taking place "on white terms" with the city's power structure maintaining control of the situation. Thus, dissenters such as Rhett James were able to challenge the Committee of 14's strategy and eventually mobilize some factions of the African-American community against the token desegregation policy.[40]

Rev. Rhett James was elected president of the Dallas NAACP in 1962 and became the most outspoken critic of the managed desegregation plan. He questioned the loyalty of the African-American members of the Committee of 14 to the African-American community. He stated unequivocally that the African-American members on the committee could not serve two masters: that is, he felt that they could not do the bidding of whites on the committee and still call themselves leaders in the African-American community. He also believed that African Americans had to win their own freedom. In his column in the *Express*, June 16, 1962, he stated: "When are we going to learn the facts of life: that we can't be Negro leaders without totally identifying with Negro causes, and remain loyal to these causes. We fool no one but ourselves if we think the Dallas School Board is going to do the right thing on their own. What has been done and what will be done comes from direct appeals, court actions and direct action from Negro movements, with all involved in them dedicated to the cause of eradicating barriers which separate some and render them inferior."[41]

Rhett James's words proved prophetic because, in spite of the Committee of 14's attempt to negotiate and manage desegregation in the city, more direct-action demonstrations occurred. In 1963, the NAACP began a selective buying campaign against the Skillern Drug stores in South Dallas because the stores would not employ African Americans, even though African Americans made up 90 percent of the customers. In 1964, African Americans and whites opposed to the slow pace of managed desegregation picketed and demonstrated at the downtown Piccadilly Cafeteria for twenty-eight consecutive days and forced the cafeteria to sign an agreement to serve all customers without regard to race. During the same year, a new organization, the Dallas Coordinating Committee on Civil Rights (DCCR), composed of members of the NAACP, SCLC, and the SNCC, picketed the Dallas school board administration building to force the school board to "broaden and accelerate school desegregation in Dallas." The biggest demonstration, however, occurred in March, 1965, when an estimated three thousand people marched and rallied in downtown to protest the killing of Rev. James Reeb in Selma, Alabama, and to support the passage of the national voting rights act.[42]

These direct-action demonstrations represented the emergence of younger, more defiant civil rights leadership in Dallas. Joining Rhett James in advocating the use of direct action was Rev. Earl E. Allen, pastor of Highland Hills Methodist Church and a leader of CORE. Rev. Allen led the pickets at the Piccadilly Cafeteria and at the school board in 1964. After leading these successful demonstrations, in August, he challenged the city council to enforce the Civil Rights Act of 1964 or face the possibility of racial unrest and violence. He also stated that if the city attempted to treat civil rights demonstrations as "criminal acts" as advocated by the Dallas Crime Commission, "blood would flow in the streets." Allen was joined in his protest of token integration in Dallas by Dudley Powell, a medical doctor and organizer of the Full Citizenship Committee. Powell's committee challenged the token school desegregation plan in operation and produced evidence that less than 160 African-American students had attended integrated schools in the first three years of the plan's operation. Overall, Powell, Allen, and other dissidents in CORE and SCLC believed that Dallas would never desegregate until African Americans used direct-action demonstrations and filed lawsuits to force change.[43]

African Americans working with the Committee of 14 continued to advocate negotiations at the bargaining table and to condemn and resist the direct-action tactics advocated by James, Powell, and Allen. Moreover, their success in achieving racial change through negotiation supported their position. In June, 1963, for example, the African-American members of the Committee of 14 announced another achievement: all swimming pools and parks in Dallas would be desegregated. One month later, they reported that all of the city's theaters would be open to all citizens. Upon making these announcements, committee president Rev. E. C. Estell, who had replaced original committee member Henry Lenoir, commended the African-American community for its self-discipline and patience during the desegregation process.[44] One year later, Rev. Estell also took the offensive against dissidents in CORE and SCLC who disagreed with the managed desegregation plan. Shortly after Allen's statement that the failure of the Dallas city council to enforce the Civil Rights Act of 1964 would cause racial unrest and violence, Rev. Estell responded by condemning direct-action tactics and calling for a moratorium on picketing in Dallas. Estell said that direct action had reached a point of "diminishing returns" and public opinion had turned against civil rights demonstrations. He called for law and order and for more sessions at the conference table in order to achieve civil rights for African Americans in Dallas.[45]

This division among African-American leadership split the civil rights movement in the city. The older, established leadership, represented by Smith, Estell, the ministers in the IMA, and African-American members of the Committee of 14, continued to advocate negotiation and gradual change. They had worked with members of the Citizens Council for years and realized some benefits for the African-American community and themselves by going along with the established way of doing things in the city's political culture. Members of CORE, SNCC, and some members of the NAACP accepted and advocated direct-action tactics, Black Nationalism, and other activist positions on black liberation that emerged among African Americans during the latter phase of the civil rights movement. Moreover, many of the activist group questioned the goodwill of the white leadership represented by the Citizens Council. After the assassination of Pres. John F. Kennedy, they joined with the national media in portraying Dallas as a "city of hate," where racial prejudice and discrimination against African Americans served as obvious examples of the failure of white leadership.[46]

After 1964, the split in African-American leadership over tactics widened. The established leadership continued to negotiate and work with white leadership for racial change and to achieve gains for African Americans. For their efforts, they received concessions from white leadership in the form of the first appointments of African-Americans to city boards and commissions. In 1967, they formed the Dallas Urban League with white business leaders, and this organization became one of the most important sources for many African Americans to find employment. In the same year, C. A. Galloway became the first African American to serve on the Dallas city council when he was appointed to serve out the unexpired term of a white councilman who had resigned. In the 1969 city council election, the Citizens' Charter Association endorsed its first African-American candidate, Committee of 14 member George Allen.[47]

Despite the successes of the established leadership in gaining these concessions, members of SCLC and CORE continued to challenge them over segregation that remained in the city. In June, 1965, for example, when A. Maceo Smith presented Dallas school superintendent W. T. White a plaque for his support of the United Negro College Fund's annual fundraising campaign, CORE chairman Stanley Gaines criticized Smith for honoring a man who "overtly and covertly had done everything in his power to block total integration of the Dallas public schools." To Gaines, Smith seemed to be rewarding White for his resistance to school desegregation and to be conveying to him the message that the African-American community had forgiven him for his intractability over integration.[48] One year later, Rev. Carroll Brown of SCLC took issue with Rev. B. L. McCormick, one of the established leaders, over his statement that Dallas did not need an ordinance prohibiting discrimination because no such problem existed in the city. Brown stated that such a claim was incorrect and that the Committee of 14 had not solved the city's racial problems; it had only succeeded in appeasing the African-American community. In addition to criticizing the established leadership for aiding the enemies of African Americans in Dallas, members of CORE also requested that the federal government suspend federal funds until the Dallas school board provided African-American children an equal education. Along with SCLC, CORE also continued to picket several downtown stores to force them to desegregate.[49]

For a brief period, the Dallas Chapter of SNCC presented the most formidable challenge to the policy of negotiating racial change in the city. In 1968, members of SNCC began a campaign to buy out white businesses in South Dallas. This campaign was an example of the emerging Black Nationalist philosophy of SNCC on the national level to empower African Americans to control their communities economically and politically. It also represented SNCC's commitment to mass organizing as a method of achieving racial change.[50] The first target of SNCC's campaign was the OK supermarket chain. When the owner refused to sell to a SNCC-sponsored group, SNCC organized a boycott of the chain and supported the boycott with daily picketing. The picketing led to an alleged "bottle-smashing raid" at one of the stores, and the police arrested two members of SNCC for destroying property. In a subsequent trial, the Dallas County prosecutor portrayed the members of SNCC as violent, black "revolutionists." A jury convicted both men on a charge of destroying property and sentenced them to ten years in jail. Several members of the African-American community testified on behalf of the two SNCC members in an attempt to refute the charge that they were violent "revolutionists." But none of the established leadership came to their defense. It also appeared that city officials had embarked on a campaign to disrupt SNCC's activities in Dallas. Subsequently, other members were accused of crimes, including one who was framed for an armed bank robbery. Fearing similar reprisals, one member of SNCC hijacked a plane to Cuba. Under these pressures, the Dallas chapter of SNCC disappeared from the city.[51]

The experience of SNCC was symbolic of how the civil rights movement in Dallas remained fractured. The established African-American leadership continued to negotiate change and to discourage mass action and demonstrations. The activists and the agitators in Dallas remained on the fringes and could not produce results nor overcome the criticism they received from the established leadership. For example, in 1969, when Peter Johnson of SCLC sought to organize a boycott of downtown restaurants and stores to protest the continuing existence of poor housing for African Americans in the Fair Park area of South Dallas, he was immediately castigated by city councilman and Committee of 14 veteran George Allen. Reminiscent of Rev. Estell's position five years earlier, Allen took issue with Johnson's methods as well as his lack of ties to the city: "I look with disfavor on an outsider coming in here who pays no taxes and who has no roots here — organizing a boycott. This is our town, we have our roots and stakes down here, we're concerned about what happens here. If you have lived here five years ago, you can see vast improvement throughout the city. Sure there are some inequities, but we need to work at this through black leadership that has been working a long time and is really getting things done."[52] Allen's criticism of the boycott and Johnson's lack of roots in the city did not stop Johnson from continuing the boycott and giving the city thirty days to respond. It became the first in a series of demonstrations that Johnson would lead to challenge A. Maceo Smith and Allen to recognize the legitimacy of direct-action protests.[53]

The two factions represented by Allen and Johnson in the city's ongoing civil rights movement did not come together until a crisis made cooperation necessary. In 1972, the Dallas police shot and killed nine African-American men and wounded eleven others in the course of several months. In addition, the Dallas police appeared to have embarked on a reign of terror in the city's African-American communities, which caused several African-American activists to criticize the police and threaten violent retaliation. To protest police violence, SCLC, under the leadership of Johnson, sponsored a march of one thousand people to city hall in October, 1972, and then held a series of demonstrations which included a school walkout, a boycott of a shopping center, and the takeover of the city council chambers and city manager's office. A coalition of community leaders and groups, which included such diverse groups as the IMA, the Urban League, the Nation of Islam, and Dallas Legal Services, formed to present the African-American community's grievances to the city council and to call for action to stop police violence. Leading the coalition was A. Maceo Smith, and it was the first time that the established leadership worked with "black activist" groups such as SCLC to address a problem confronting African Americans in Dallas.[54]

Speaking for the coalition, Smith addressed the City Council on November 20, 1972. In his speech he cited his long history of community service and warned the council of the potential of violence if it did not address the police problem. Smith stated that he represented twenty-eight African-American organizations from all ranges of the political spectrum. He presented eleven demands of the coalition, which included the establishment of a community relations commission to investigate complaints against the police, the hiring of more African-American police officers, the appointment of an African-American deputy police chief, and the assignment of African-American police officers to the African-American community.[55]

Smith's appearance before the council produced results. Since he represented the established leadership that had worked with the city's white leadership for over thirty years, the council was more than willing to respond to his demands for action to forestall potential violence. Moreover, the demonstrations organized by SCLC provided him a better bargaining position. At the request of the city council, the chief of police called upon Smith and other members of the coalition to assist in improving the relationship between the police and African Americans. The chief of police also developed a strategy to recruit more

African-American police officers and to address the demands cited by Smith and the coalition in Smith's speech to the council. Acting on the coalition's demands, the police department appointed its first African-American deputy police chief in 1973. The key development, however, was that Smith, and other African Americans and organizations representing the established leadership, finally joined with those who advocated direct-action tactics to use both negotiations and direct action to achieve social and political change for African Americans in Dallas.[56]

The coalition led by Smith was short-lived. In fact, Smith's speech before the city council in November, 1972, was one of his last major acts as a leader of African Americans in Dallas. He died in 1977.[57] After the 1972 coalition, African-American activists such as Peter Johnson and Al Lipscomb moved to the forefront of the city's African-American leadership. They proceeded to use the methods and tactics that African Americans in other parts of the South had used to win their political and economic rights. They demonstrated, filed lawsuits, and used other confrontational methods in an effort to win the political and economic gains that African Americans in cities such as Atlanta and Birmingham had already obtained. They also attempted to overcome the politics of "accommodation" that had dominated the civil rights movement in Dallas in the 1960s.[58]

The ascendancy of activists after 1972 was a clear indication of the limits of negotiation to achieve racial change. The continuation of racial segregation in education and in housing were additional examples of the limited success of the civil rights movement in Dallas. The current conflict over the access of African Americans and Hispanics to political and economic power in the city is another sign of the failure of negotiated racial change. Nevertheless, Smith, Estell, and their generation of African-American leadership played what they thought was their best hand. They had worked with members of the Citizens Council for over twenty years and knew how white leadership in the city "got things done." As a result, they bypassed the mass organizing and direct-action tactics used by African Americans in other southern cities to achieve racial change. The mass organizing in other cities not only broke down the barriers of racial segregation, but also mobilized African Americans at the grass-roots level to participate in the political process. The decision by African-American leadership to negotiate racial change prevented this phenomenon from occurring in Dallas. As a result, a legacy of apathy now exists among the city's African-American population, and it has forestalled mobilizing them even for causes and issues which directly affect them.

NOTES

1. For news coverage of the continuing racial conflict in Dallas, see the *Dallas Morning News,* Feb. 2, 1986, Dec. 9, 1989, Aug. 26, 1990, Sept. 19, 1990, May 8, 1991; Laura Miller, "The Hustler," *D Magazine*, Mar., 1991, pp. 41–45, 70–72.

2. Jim Schutze, *The Accommodation: The Politics of Race in an American City* (Secaucus, New Jersey: Citadel Press, 1987). See my review of this study in the *Southwestern Historical Quarterly* 93 (Jan., 1990): 419–20.

3. For some of the recent interpretations of various aspects and goals of the civil rights movement, see Taylor Branch, *Parting the Waters: America in the King Years, 1954–63* (New York: Simon & Schuster, 1988); David Garrow, *Bearing the Cross: Martin Luther King, Jr. and the Southern Christian Leadership Conference* (New York: William Morrow & Co., 1986); Stephen B. Oates, *Let the Trumpet Sound: The Life of Martin Luther King, Jr.* (New York: Harper & Row, 1982); Genna Rae McNeil, *Groundwork: Charles Hamilton Houston and the Struggle for Civil Rights* (Philadelphia: University of Pennsylvania Press, 1983); Richard Kluger, *Simple Justice: The History of Brown vs. Board of Education and Black America's Struggle for Equality* (New York: Alfred A. Knopf, 1976); Steven Lawson, *Black Ballots: Voting Rights in the South, 1944–1969* (New York: Columbia University Press, 1976); Darlene Clark Hine, *Black Victory: The Rise and Fall of the White Primary in Texas* (Millwood, N.Y.: KTO Press, 1979); James Farmer, *Lay Bare the Heart: An Autobiography of the Civil Rights Movement* (New York: Arbor House, 1985); and James Forman, *The Making of Black Revolutionaries* (Washington, D.C.: Open Hand Publishing, 1985). Two studies pertinent and comparable to this one are David Garrow, *Protest at Selma: Martin Luther King, Jr. and the Voting Rights Act of 1965* (New Haven, Conn.: Yale University Press, 1978); and William H. Chafe, *Civilities and Civil Liberties: Greensboro, North Carolina and the Black Struggle for Freedom* (New York: Oxford University Press, 1980).

4. For this interpretation of race relations in Texas, see Chandler Davidson, *Biracial Politics: Conflict and Coalition in the Metropolitan South* (Baton Rouge: Louisiana State University Press, 1972); and Robert A. Goldberg, "Racial Change on the Southern Periphery: The Case of San Antonio, Texas, 1960–1965," *Journal of Southern History* 49 (Aug., 1983): 349–74. John G. Sproat, "Perspectives on Desegregation in South Carolina," in Robert H. Abzug and Stephen E. Maizlish, eds., *New Perspectives on Race and Slavery in America* (Lexington: University of Kentucky Press, 1986), pp. 164–84, offers a similar interpretation for how desegregation took place in South Carolina's major cities.

5. For an assessment of the violence against African Americans in this period, see Barry Crouch, "A Spirit of Lawlessness: White Violence, Texas Blacks, 1865–1868," *Journal of Social History* 18 (Winter, 1984): 217–32. For the actual records of violence against African Americans during the period, see *Records of Criminal Offenses Committed in the State of Texas*, Sept., 1865–Dec., 1868, Roll 32, Records of the Assistant

Commissioner for the State of Texas, Bureau of Refugees, Freedmen & Abandoned Lands, 1865–1869, National Archives, Washington, D.C.

6. *Dallas Morning News*, Mar. 4, 1910: Dallas *Times Herald*, March 3, 4, 5, 1910; Herbert Shapiro, *White Violence and Black Response: From Reconstruction to Montgomery* (Amherst: University of Massachusetts Press, 1988), pp. 111–12.

7. *New York Tribune*, Apr. 3, 1921; *Chicago Whip*, Apr. 9, 1921. A list of KKK members on the Dallas police department was found in a letter from Earl Bieser, San Diego Chapter of the Knights of the Invisible Empire, to Ben E. Cabell, Aug. 13, 1921, Correspondence; Earle Cabell Papers, Box 1. The Cabell Papers are located in the DeGolyer Collection at Southern Methodist University, Dallas, Tex.

8. Merline Pitre, *Through Many Dangers, Toils and Snares: Black Leadership in Texas, 1868–1900* (Austin, Tex.: Eakin Press, 1985); James M. Smallwood, *The Struggle for Equality: Blacks in Texas* (Boston: American Press, 1983), p. 18; Donald Strong, "The Poll Tax: The Case of Texas," *American Political Science Review* 38 (Aug., 1944): 693–709; Darlene Clark Hine, "The Elusive Ballot: The Black Struggle Against the Texas Democratic White Primary, 1932–1945," *Southwestern Historical Quarterly* 81 (Apr., 1978): 371–92; Robert B. Fairbanks, "Dallas in the 1940s: The Challenges and Opportunities of Defense Mobilization," in Char Miller and Heywood Sanders, eds., *Urban Texas: Politics and Development* (College Station: Texas A&M University Press, 1990), pp. 141–43; and Robert B. Fairbanks, "The Good Government Machine: The Citizens Charter Association and Dallas Politics, 1930–1960," in Robert B. Fairbanks and Kathleen Underwood, eds., *Essays on Sunbelt Cities and Recent Urban America* (College Station: Texas A&M University Press, 1990), p. 127. Information on how the apartheid system was erected in Dallas is found in the case, *Lipscomb* v. *Wise*, CA 3-4571-E (1975). For an analysis of segregation in Texas, see Bruce A. Glasrud, "Jim Crow's Emergence in Texas," *American Studies* 15 (Spring, 1974): 47–60.

9. For the leadership of A. S. Jackson and Ammon S. Wells in Dallas's African-American community, see the *Dallas Express*, Nov. 1, 15, 1919, Jan. 24, 1920, May 8, 1920, Jan. 17, 1936, Feb. 22, 1936; and Peter W. Agnew, "Making Dallas Moral: Two Baptist Pastors," *Heritage News* 12 (Summer, 1987): 19–25. For examples of petitions submitted by African Americans in Dallas, see City of Dallas, *Minute Book*, 8 (May 26, 1888), p. 150, *Minute Book*, 23 (Sept. 26, 1896), p. 260; *Dallas Express*, Sept. 18, 1920. For the founding of the NAACP in Dallas, see the *Dallas Express*, Oct. 4, 1947, May 28, 1949, Mar. 15, 1952; Michael L. Gillette, "The Rise of the NAACP in Texas," *Southwestern Historical Quarterly* 81 (Apr., 1978): 393–98.

10. "The Black Community in Early Dallas," Dallas County Heritage Society pamphlet, n.d.; Thomas H. Smith, "'Cast Down Your Bucket': A Black Experiment in Dallas," *Heritage News* 12 (Spring, 1987): 13–18; Mamie McKnight, ed., *First African American Families of Dallas: Creative Survival*, vol. 1 (Dallas: Black Dallas Remembered Steering Committee, 1987); Tempie V. Strange, "The Dallas Negro Chamber of Commerce: A Study of a Negro Institution," (Master's thesis, Southern Methodist University, 1945); *Pittsburgh Courier*, June 12, 1926; *Dallas Express*, Jan. 7, 1928.

11. *Dallas Express*, Feb. 25, 1928, Mar. 30, and May 11, 1935; *Dallas Morning News*, Jan. 4, 1929, July 29, 1934, Nov. 14, 1935; Robert B. Fairbanks, "From Consensus to Controversy: The Rise and Fall of Public Housing in Dallas," *Legacies* 1 (Fall, 1989): 37–43.

12. *Dallas Express*, Jan. 19, 1935, June 8, 1935, Oct. 10, 1936, Nov. 4, 1939. "Dallas Negro Chamber of Commerce History," n.d., six pages, in the Dallas Negro Chamber

of Commerce Collection, Texas-Dallas Collection, Dallas Public Library; Gillette, "Rise of NAACP," pp. 393–400. See also a letter of introduction for Smith written by his former employer in Oklahoma City, Albon L. Holsey, Executive Secretary, the National Negro Business League, to Dr. R. T. Hamilton of Dallas, Dec. 28, 1932, A. Maceo Smith Papers, in the possession of his widow, Mrs. Fannie Smith, Dallas.

13. *Dallas Morning News*, July 20, 24, 1934; *Dallas Express*, Apr. 27, 1935, and May 2, 1942. The origins of the PVL are also explained in a letter from L. Virgil Williams, executive secretary of the Dallas Negro Chamber of Commerce, to Miss Mildred Montgomery of Prairie View, Texas, Apr. 20, 1942, Correspondence, Negro Chamber of Commerce Collection, Box 1, Dallas Public Library, Dallas. See also W. Marvin Dulaney, "The Progressive Voters League," *Legacies* 3 (Spring, 1991): 27–35.

14. *Dallas Morning News*, Feb. 24, and Mar. 1, 1935; *Dallas Express*, Mar. 2, 9, 16, 23, 30, 1935; J. Mason Brewer, *Negro Legislators of Texas and Their Descendants: A History of the Negro in Texas Politics from Reconstruction to Disfranchisement* (Dallas: Mathis Publishing Co., 1935), pp. 118–19. A sample ballot containing all sixty names for the Place 3, State Representative seat can be found in the Minnie A. Flanagan Papers, an uncatalogued manuscript collection at the Dallas Historical Society. For the statewide controversy that Wells's candidacy engendered, see Dale Miller, "Should Negroes Vote in Democratic Primaries?" *Texas Weekly*, Apr. 6, 1935, pp. 1–3.

15. *Dallas Express*, Jan. 25, 1936, Feb. 1, 1936, Oct. 10, 31, 1936, Dec. 5, 12, 19, 26, 1936, Jan. 9, 1937, Mar. 27, 1937, Apr. 3, 10, 17, 1937, May 1, 1937, May 2, 1942; "Progressive Voters League," *Applause Magazine*, Sept., 1946; Williams to Montgomery, Apr. 20, 1942; *Dallas Morning News*, May 3, 1973.

16. *Dallas Express*, Mar. 7, 1936, June 12, 19, 26, 1937, July 24, 1937, Jan. 1, 1938; Gillette, "Rise of NAACP," pp. 394–400.

17. *Dallas Express*, Apr. 8, 1944; *Nixon* v. *Herndon*, 273 U.S. 536 (1927); *Nixon* v. *Condon*, 286 U.S. 73 (1932); *Grovey* v. *Townsend*, 295 U.S. 45 (1935); Conrey Bryson, *Dr. Lawrence A. Nixon and the White Primary*, Southwestern Studies No. 42 (El Paso, 1974); Hine, "The Elusive Ballot," pp. 374–90.

18. *U.S.* v. *Classic*, 313 U.S. 299 (1941); *Smith* v. *Allwright*, 321 U.S. 640 (1944); Gillette, "Rise of NAACP," pp. 400–405; Hine, *Black Victory*, pp. 215–25; *Dallas Express*, Apr. 8, 1944; *New York Times*, Apr. 4, 1944; H. M. Morgan of Dallas to Thurgood Marshall, Jan. 4, 1944, and W. J. Durham to Ed Dudley, assistant general counsel of the NAACP, Apr. 14, 1944, both in the Papers of the NAACP, Part 4, The Voting Rights of Campaign, 1916–1950, Reel 11, microform copy in Minority Cultures Collection, University of Texas at Arlington.

19. Minutes of the Dallas Council of Negro Organizations, Oct. 6, 1942, and Memo to the Texas Council of Negro Organizations, "Report of Activities" of the Dallas Council of Negro Organizations, Mar. 27, 1943, both in the Negro Chamber Collection, Box 7; *Dallas Express*, Jan. 30, 1943, Feb. 27, 1943, Mar. 6, 1943.

20. Gillette, "Rise of NAACP," p. 405; *Dallas Express*, Mar. 23, 1946, May 18, 1946; *Dallas Morning News*, May 3, 1973.

21. *Sweatt* v. *Painter et al.*, 339 U.S. 629 (1950); Kluger, *Simple Justice*, pp. 262–66, 274–84; *Dallas Express*, June 17, 1950; Michael L. Gillette, "Blacks Challenge the White University," *Southwestern Historical Quarterly* 86 (Oct. 1982): 321–44.

22. *Dallas Express*, Aug. 8, 1941, Aug. 3, 10, 1946, Nov. 9, 1946, Feb. 8, 1947; *Dallas Morning News*, Oct. 31, 1946, Mar. 25, 1947; Dallas Negro Chamber of Commerce, *Negro City Directory, 1947–1948* (Dallas, 1948), pp. 35–44; "Monthly Report of the Executive Secretary to the Board of Directors, Negro Chamber of Commerce,"

Jan. 7, 1943, Dallas Negro Chamber of Commerce Collection, Box 1. For the council authorization of fourteen African-American police officers, see City of Dallas Council, *Minute Book*, 65, Oct. 17, 1946, p. 367, and Oct. 30, 1946, p. 467.

23. Fairbanks, "From Consensus to Controversy," pp. 37–43; Schutze, *Accommodation*, pp. 1–26, 67–74; *Dallas Express*, Mar. 29, 1941, May 24, 1941, Nov. 29, 1941, Feb. 8, 1950 through Nov. 25, 1950, June 30, 1951, July 7, 1951, July 21, 1951, May 2, 1953, July 25, 1953, Nov. 14, 1953; *Dallas Star Post*, Sept. 29, 1951; Juanita Craft to Walter White, Aug. 4, 1951, Juanita Craft Collection, Texas-Dallas Collection, Dallas Public Library; "Racial Dynamism in Dallas," *New Republic*, Mar. 24, 1941, pp. 398–90.

24. *Dallas Express*, Sept. 11, 1954, Aug. 27, 1955, Sept. 10, 17, 24, 1955, Oct. 8, 1955, June 23, 1956, Aug. 11, 1956, Sept. 15, 1956, Oct. 27, 1956, June 1, 1957, July 27, 1957, Aug. 24, 31, 1957, Sept. 14, 1957, Jan. 4, 1958, Aug. 1, 8, 1959, Oct. 10, 1959, Feb. 27, 1960, Mar. 19, 1960, Apr. 16, 1960, May 21, 1960, June 4, 1960.

25. The Texas Citizens Council of Dallas should not be confused with the Dallas Citizens Council. For the formation of the former organization, see the *Dallas Morning News*, Aug. 21, 1955, Aug. 31, 1955; *Dallas Express*, July 30, 1955.

26. *Dallas Express*, Sept. 22, 29, 1956, Oct. 6, 13, 20, 27, 1956, Nov. 3, 17, 1956, Apr. 27, 1957, May 25, 1957. See also the petition, *State of Texas* v. *the NAACP et al.*, Civil Action 56–649, Sept. 22, 1956, which named A. Maceo Smith and other Texas NAACP members as defendants.

27. *Dallas Express*, July 27, 1957, Dec. 13, 1958, Jan. 3, 1959, Mar. 14, 21, 1959, Mar. 5, 1960, Mar. 12, 1960. Smith's letter of resignation from the NAACP is in his papers. See A. Maceo Smith to Channing Tobias, Chairman of the Board, NAACP, May 15, 1957. The *Dallas Express*, May 25, 1957, also reported his resignation. For the reaction of his superiors at the FHA to his being named in the state's case against the NAACP, see W. Richard Lomax, Director of Personnel, FHA, to A. Maceo Smith, Sept. 25, 1956, Smith Papers.

28. A. C. Greene, *Dallas U.S.A.* (Austin: Texas Monthly Press, 1984), pp. 38–39; "Negroes Militant," *Texas Observer*, Mar. 11, 1960, pp. 1, 3; *Dallas Morning News*, Aug. 1, 5, 7, 1960, Aug. 26, 1961; *Dallas Times Herald*, May 25, 1961, Sept. 6, 7, 1961; *Dallas Express*, Feb. 27, 1960, Mar. 12, 20, 1960, May 28, 1960, Aug. 13, 1960, Sept. 24, 1960, Oct. 1, 1960, Dec. 10, 1960, Aug. 12, 1961, Sept. 9, 1961. Three years after the plan was implemented, the Southern Regional Council lauded the Dallas desegregation plan. See "Texas: Pace Increases in Last Part of Decade," *Southern School News: Ten Years in Review*, May 17, 1964, p. 14, in the Papers of Dr. Martin Luther King, Box 140, Martin Luther King Jr. Center for Nonviolent Social Change, Atlanta, Georgia.

29. Fairbanks, "Good Government Machine," pp. 125–47; Richard A. Smith, "How Business Failed Dallas," *Fortune*, 1964, pp. 156–63; *New York Times*, Jan. 19, 1964.

30. The beginnings of the negotiations for desegregation in Dallas were noted in Margaret Price, "Toward A Solution of the Sit-In Controversy," Southern Regional Council Special Report, May, 31, 1960, p. 16, King Papers, Box 140; *Dallas Express*, Oct. 8, 1960; *Dallas Morning News*, July 5, 1964. See also the transcript of an interview with A. Maceo Smith by Sam Cameron, Nov. 13, 1972, Fisk University Library Oral History Program, pp. 7–8. For a retrospective look at the impact of Wilkins's visit in 1960, see a letter from H. Rhett James, president, Dallas Metropolitan Council, NAACP, to A. Maceo Smith, Mar. 30, 1972. Both of the preceding documents are in the Smith Papers.

31. Remarks of A. Maceo Smith before the Joint Committee of the Dallas Citizens Council and Negro Leadership, Mar. 24, 1960, Smith Papers.

32. *Dallas Express*, Apr. 30, 1960, Oct. 8, 15, 22, 1960.

33. *Dallas Express*, Nov. 12, 26, 1960, Dec. 17, 1960.

34. *Dallas Express*, Jan. 7, 14, 1961, Mar. 4, 1961, May 27, 1961.

35. A. Maceo Smith to Rev. E. C. Estell, June 7, 1961, Smith Papers.

36. Ibid.; *Dallas Express*, Aug. 5, 1961; *Dallas Morning News*, July 7, 1964.

37. *Dallas Express*, Aug. 12, 1961; *Dallas Morning News*, July 7, 1964. The African-American members of the Committee of 14 assumed responsibility for showing and discussing the film with African-American audiences. A copy of the script that A. Maceo Smith used to introduce the film and a booklet on the film are in the Smith Papers.

38. *Dallas Express*, Aug. 19, 1961; Schutze, *Accommodation*, pp. 128–39; *Dallas Morning News*, July 5, 6, 7, 10, 1964. As early as 1960, when the plan was being implemented, the Southern Regional Council lauded it. See Price, "Toward A Solution to the Sit-In Controversy," p. 16.

39. Smith to Estell, June 7, 1961; *Dallas Express*, Oct. 22, 1960, Aug. 26, 1961, Mar. 10, 24, 31, 1962, June 16, 1962, Dec. 29, 1962.

40. Greene, *Dallas U.S.A.*; Schutze, *Accommodation*. The climate of "managing desegregation" in Dallas was so tight that even Dr. Martin Luther King, Jr., was unwelcome in the city during 1963 and 1964. The committee attempted to block King's appearance at a political rally sponsored by Rhett James and the United Political Organization in January, 1963, but failed. See the *Dallas Express*, Jan. 5, 1963, and Mar. 2, 1963; *Dallas Times Herald*, Jan. 2, 1963. The committee was successful in blocking King's appearance at Southern Methodist University in March, 1964, and the SMU Student Association had to rescind its invitation to King to speak on campus. See John A. Hill, president of the Student Association, Southern Methodist University, to Dr. Martin Luther King, Jr., Mar. 18, 1964; Dr. Dudley V. Powell of Dallas to Dr. Martin Luther King, Jr., Apr. 16, 1964. Both letters are in the King Papers, Box 57. The charge that desegregation in Dallas was taking place "on white terms" was made by an African-American respondent to a study done in 1964: see Lewis W. Jones and Herman H. Long, *The Negotiation of Desegregation in Ten Southern Cities* (Nashville, Tenn.: Fisk University, 1965), pp. 28–29.

41. *Dallas Express*, June 16, 1962.

42. *Dallas Express*, Apr. 13, 20, 27, 1963, May 11, 1963, Mar. 20, 27, 1965; *Dallas Times Herald*, June 28, 1964; *Dallas Morning News*, Apr. 28, 1964, Mar. 5, 1965; *Dallas Post Tribune*, June 6, 20, 1964.

43. *Dallas Times Herald*, June 28, 1964, Aug. 18, 1964; Powell to King, Apr. 16, 1964; *Dallas Post Tribune*, Aug. 29, 1964.

44. *Dallas Express*, June 22, 1963, July 7, 1963.

45. *Dallas Morning News*, Aug. 23, 1964; *Dallas Morning News*, Aug. 23, 1964. Estell and Allen debated the issue of the effectiveness of direct-action tactics in the *Dallas Post Tribune*, Aug. 29, 1964.

46. Fairbanks, "The Good Government Machine," p. 146; *Dallas Express*, June 8, 1963, Nov. 30, 1963, Dec. 14, 1963; *Dallas Post Tribune*, Jan. 4, 18, 1964, Feb. 15, 22, 1964. For a very insightful comment on the failure of white leadership in Dallas following the Kennedy assassination, see a speech by John Leslie Patton, principal of Booker T. Washington High School and an African American who would have been considered a member of Dallas's "established black leadership," entitled "Our City Dallas—Its Image," delivered at the opening of Pinkston High School, Nov. 4, 1964, copy in Smith Papers.

47. For articles that show how white leadership began to include African Americans

on decision-making boards and commissions and appoint them to judgeships and political office in Dallas, see the *Dallas Express*, Apr. 3, 1965, June 5, 1965, Aug. 28, 1965, Feb. 9, 1966, Feb. 19, 1966 (on this date, former dissenter Rhett James accepted an appointment to the city Board of Solicitation), July 23, 1966, Jan. 7, 1967, Feb. 25, 1967, Nov. 16, 1968. For the founding of the Urban League in Dallas, see the *Dallas Express*, June 24, 1967, Urban League folder, Smith Papers.

48. *Dallas Express*, June 19, 26, 1965.

49. *Dallas Express*, Aug. 7, 14, 1965, Apr. 16, 1966.

50. For the political stance of SNCC after 1966, see Forman, *Making of Black Revolutionaries*, pp. 433–47; and Cleveland Sellers with Robert Terrell, *The River of No Return: The Autobiography of A Black Militant and the Life and Death of SNCC* (New York: William Morrow & Co., 1972), pp. 170–72. For the importance of the methodology of mass organizing, see Aldon Morris, *The Origins of the Civil Rights Movement: Black Communities Organizing for Change* (New York: Free Press, 1984), pp. ix–xiv.

51. For information on the Dallas chapter of SNCC and its troubles, see the *Dallas Express*, July 20, 1968, July 27, 1968, Aug. 10, 1968; *Dallas Morning News*, Aug. 24, 1968; *Dallas Post Tribune*, July 31, 1968; my interview with Fahim Minkah, Mar. 8, 1991, taped; "Dear Brother and Sisters," letter from Ernest McMillan, director, Dallas SNCC, Mar. 11, 1968, SNCC Papers, Box 24, King Center, Atlanta.

52. *Dallas Express*, Dec. 13, 20, 1969.

53. *Dallas Express*, Aug. 1, 22, 1970; "Editorial," *Today's Black World Magazine*, Mar. 19–25, 1971, p. 14, copy in Smith Papers.

54. *Dallas Morning News*, Nov. 26, 1972; *Dallas Times Herald*, Nov. 21, 1972; Speech by A. Maceo Smith to the Dallas City Council, Nov. 21, 1972, transcript. Attached to the transcript of the speech was a list of the twenty–eight member organizations of the coalition.

55. Smith speech to Dallas City Council, Nov. 21, 1972. As early as 1967, Smith had expressed some disillusionment with the progress of racial change in Dallas as a result of the work of the Committee of 14. See *Dallas Morning News*, Oct. 2, 1967. The shootings of 1972 made him more willing to support the stance of the activists and seem to have provided him the opportunity. Ironically, the city of Dallas had formed a Greater Dallas Community Relations Commission in 1969. Consisting of members from the Dallas Citizens Council, the Black Chamber of Commerce, and the League of United Latin American Citizens, it functioned like every other official organization in Dallas—to control dissent and "prevent problems." *Dallas Express*, Feb. 1, 1969.

56. Memorandum: George R. Schrader, acting city manager, to the Honorable Mayor and Members of the City Council, Dec. 18, 1972, on the subject of Law Enforcement in the Black Community, and Frank Dyson, chief of police, Dallas, Texas, to A. Maceo Smith, Jan. 18, 1973, both in Smith Papers; *Dallas Morning News*, Dec. 19, 1972; *Dallas Post Tribune*, June 26, 1982.

57. *Dallas Morning News.*, Dec. 20, 1977.

58. There are numerous examples of how the shift in leadership style among African Americans in Dallas spurred more direct-action tactics. See the following sampling: "The All American City," *Today's Black World Magazine*, Mar. 19–25, 1971, p. 14; Steve Kenny, "The Struggle for Power," *D Magazine*, June, 1981, pp. 98–101, 136–44; *Dallas Observer*, July 13, 1989; *Dallas Morning News*, July 29, 1990.

activists of the movement in Mississippi from 1965 to 1968, to show what happened after the famous Freedom Summer of 1964, which attracted national attention. George C. Wright shows how African Americans in Kentucky from 1900 to 1970 faced the same racial restrictions and violence as blacks in Mississippi, Georgia, and Alabama. W. Marvin Dulaney traces the rise and fall of the movement in Dallas, Texas, from the 1930s through the 1970s, while the nation's attention was focused elsewhere.

These essays exemplify the enormous range of possibilities for innovative scholarship on the subject and ensure that the civil rights movement will remain one of the most intellectually exciting areas of historical research.

Volume editors W. Marvin Dulaney, assistant professor, and Kathleen Underwood, associate professor, both teach history at the University of Texas at Arlington.